Attracting External Funds for Continuing Education

John H. Buskey, *Editor*

NEW DIRECTIONS FOR CONTINUING EDUCATION

ALAN B. KNOX, *Editor-in-Chief*

Number 12, December 1981

Paperback sourcebooks in
The Jossey-Bass Higher Education Series

Jossey-Bass Inc., Publishers
San Francisco • Washington • London

Attracting External Funds for Continuing Education
Number 12, December 1981
    John H. Buskey, *Editor*

New Directions for Continuing Education Series
Alan B. Knox, *Editor-in-Chief*

New Directions for Continuing Education (publication number
USPS 493-930) quarterly by Jossey-Bass Inc., Publishers.
Second-class postage rates paid at San Francisco, California,
and at additional mailing offices.

Correspondence:
Subscriptions, single-issue orders, change of address notices,
undelivered copies, and other correspondence should be sent to
New Directions Subscriptions, Jossey-Bass Inc., Publishers,
433 California Street, San Francisco, California 94104.

Editorial correspondence should be sent to the Editor-in-Chief,
Alan B. Knox, Teacher Education Building, Room 264,
University of Wisconsin, 225 North Mills Street, Madison,
Wisconsin 53706.

Library of Congress Catalogue Card Number LC 80-84270
International Standard Serial Number ISSN 0195-2242
International Standard Book Number ISBN 87589-819-X

Cover art by Willi Baum
Manufactured in the United States of America

Ordering Information

The paperback sourcebooks listed below are published quarterly and can be ordered either by subscription or as single copies.

Subscriptions cost $30.00 per year for institutions, agencies, and libraries. Individuals can subscribe at the special rate of $18.00 per year *if payment is by personal check.* (Note that the full rate of $30.00 applies if payment is by institutional check, even if the subscription is designated for an individual.) Standing orders are accepted.

Single copies are available at $6.95 when payment accompanies order, and *all single-copy orders under $25.00 must include payment.* (California, Washington, D.C., New Jersey, and New York residents please include appropriate sales tax.) For billed orders, cost per copy is $6.95 plus postage and handling. (Prices subject to change without notice.)

To ensure correct and prompt delivery, all orders must give either the *name of an individual* or an *official purchase order number.* Please submit your order as follows:

Subscriptions: specify series and subscription year.
Single Copies: specify sourcebook code and issue number (such as, CE8).

Mail orders for United States and Possessions, Latin America, Canada, Japan, Australia, and New Zealand to:
Jossey-Bass Inc., Publishers
433 California Street
San Francisco, California 94104

Mail orders for all other parts of the world to:
Jossey-Bass Limited
28 Banner Street
London EC1Y 8QE

New Directions for Continuing Education Series
Alan B. Knox, *Editor-in-Chief*

Contents

Editor's Notes

Most continuing education organizations never seem to have enough money and staff to provide all the programs and services they would like to offer. As a result, many organizations seek additional funds and resources in the form of grants and contracts from both the public sector and private sector. In a time of scarcity, organizations that have never before sought external funding are now seeking information and skills necessary for success in an increasingly competitive marketplace.

This sourcebook will help continuing education administrators secure external support for their endeavors, whether they practice their profession in colleges and universities, municipal, county or state government agencies, consulting firms, voluntary community agencies, public schools, community education programs, or corporations. By external support, we mean supplementary funding for special projects or purposes that allows continuing education administrators to provide programs or services that are not possible without special external resources. We have not concerned ourselves with the basic funding support of continuing education organizations—be it income from student or participant fees, regular allocations from a parent organization, or standard tax funds.

Because continuing education administrators work in different types of agencies, their programming shows diversity and variety, and includes training and instructional programs, counseling and advising, career guidance, selected applied research activities, and various other services for adults of all ages. The authors of this sourcebook, therefore, have tried to reflect this diversity in writing about the processes, procedures, and opportunities related to seeking external funding.

This sourcebook provides an overview of the processes involved in securing external funding for continuing education organizations. It is organized into three major sections. In the first chapter, "A Process Approach to Proposal Development," Richard Maybee provides an overview of a systematic process for developing proposals and describes the four major phases of concept development, proposal writing, funding agency review, and project operation. In a major sense, it provides a base for the scope of the rest of the volume.

The next seven chapters describe in detail the major steps in the process outlined in chapter one. Frank Adams writes about ways to use standardized components that are common to most proposals. By increasing the efficiency of the proposal-writing process, the number of proposals produced can be increased significantly. Twila Liggett, in the chapter on "Funding Sources," tells how to find out where the money is. She discusses

1

the three major sources of funds, what documents are available, how to conduct research, and how to do computer searches.

In "Writing the Proposal," Richard Maybee suggests an unusual, and probably unique, sequence to use in preparing the individual components of a proposal. He also proposes the use of continuity worksheets as an aid to maintaining consistency within the proposal, and his tips for writers will be helpful even to the experienced grants seeker.

Many people have difficulty with budgeting, however, Lynn Willett's chapter on "Project Budgeting" describes a step-by-step process for budget development, and presents an example of a budget. He makes the point that a budget is simply a summary of a proposal expressed in terms of dollars.

The next two chapters deal with the review processes that different agencies use in evaluating proposals. Donald Deppe, author of "What Government Agencies Look for in Proposals," describes the nature of review processes in federal and state agencies. John Buskey, in "What Foundations Look for in Proposals," describes how foundations should be approached, and the processes they use to evaluate proposals.

The last phase of the development process, managing and operating the funded project, is discussed by Lynn Willett. He describes the funded project as a *temporary* organization (usually within a parent or permanent organization) that is subject to the pitfalls of late start-ups, early staff departures, and numerous regulations.

The third section of the book presents a series of special topics related to both technical matters and additional sources of funds. William Flowers and John Harris discuss "The Multiplier Effect," a concept long known in the field of economics, which they apply to the field of continuing education. Their main point is that one grant or contract can, and should, be used as the basis for building organizational competencies and capabilities that will secure other funds.

Continuing education administrators in the past have tended to focus most of their attention on the acquisition of grants. In "Contracting," Frank Adams discusses sources of additional opportunities for providing services to clients and funding for programs. He notes the differences between contracts and grants and describes how to submit bids for contracts.

Under the rubric of "there's no such thing as a free lunch," Stanley Matelski discusses the full range of federal laws and regulations, and their impact on recipients of federal grants and contracts.

In the next chapter, Maurice Atkinson points out how "Fund Raising for Continuing Education" differs from contract and grant proposal writing. He suggests that continuing education organizations have certain unique qualities that may be very attractive to potential donors.

External funding, contracts and grants, fund raising, or grantsmanship—whatever phrase one chooses to use—has generated its own terminology and jargon, which may be confusing, if not unintelligible, to the neophyte. Thus, with the help of several others, I have compiled a glossary of terms relating to external funding that may be helpful in finding one's way through the myriad opportunities that await the enterprising proposal writer.

It was not possible to include in this volume all topics that have some bearing on externally funded programs. Evaluation is one such topic, for it is a concern with most projects and needs to be addressed in nearly every proposal. The reader who wishes to pursue the subject in greater depth is referred to *New Directions for Continuing Education: Assessing the Impact of Continuing Education*, no. 3, by Alan B. Knox (1979), *New Directions for Program Evaluation: Evaluating Federally Sponsored Programs*, no. 2, by Charlotte C. Rentz and R. Robert Rentz (1978), and other volumes in the Jossey-Bass sourcebook series *New Directions for Program Evaluation*, edited by Scarvia B. Anderson.

When this book was first conceived, there were few hints that the federal and state government funding picture would change as dramatically as it has over such a short period of time. As this volume goes to press, it is clear that we are in an era of change, and unfortunately our vision, collectively and individually, is still somewhat unclear as to the future levels of funding and the purposes for which funding may be available. Nevertheless, several authors have suggested what they surmise the future may be. Individually, they differ in their projections, yet each seems credible given a particular perspective. In truth, they may all be correct about the future, for different funding agencies may adopt different strategies. There will be change; how much, and in what specific directions are questions for which definitive answers are not yet available. In any event, skill in seeking external funds will continue to be an important element in the success of continuing education administrators.

John H. Buskey
Editor

References

Knox, A. B. (Ed.). *New Directions for Continuing Education: Assessing the Impact of Continuing Education,* no. 3. San Francisco: Jossey-Bass, 1979.
Rentz, C. C., and Rentz, R. R. (Eds.). *New Directions for Program Evaluation: Evaluating Federally Sponsored Programs,* no. 2. San Francisco: Jossey-Bass, 1978.

John H. Buskey is associate dean of continuing studies and assistant professor of adult and continuing education at the University of Nebraska-Lincoln. He has had nearly fifteen years' experience as a proposal writer and project director, and regularly conducts workshops and seminars on proposal writing and grantsmanship.

*The process of proposal development need not be as
overwhelming as it may appear at first glance. By
breaking the process into workable parts, increased
understanding as well as greater effectiveness can
occur in managing proposal development from
beginning to end.*

A Process Approach
to Proposal Development

Richard G. Maybee

Grants and contracts are not for everyone. Depending on the funding
source, project proposals can be long and detailed. Some organizations are
prepared to both write proposals and manage projects. Others have difficulty doing one or the other or both. The question is—how do you know if
your organization should seek grants and contracts? There are several
considerations.

External Funds for Significant Support. If your organization relies
too heavily on external project funds, there is a risk of cutbacks due to
funding agency priority changes. The Reagan administration cutbacks in
1981 in social service funding should serve as a clear example of this
problem. Further, organizational continuity can be in constant jeopardy
when external funds must be sought year after year in order to keep basic
functions operating. Organizational ups and downs such as those resulting
from successes and failures in the competitive field of grant seeking can also
add to weakened organizational credibility, so vital to obtaining external
funds in the first place. Organizations that develop a broad funding base
from individuals, the community, corporations, foundations, and government funds will have a greater chance of remaining stable and viable
over the long term.

J. Buskey (Ed.). *New Directions for Continuing Education: Attracting External Funds
for Continuing Education,* no. 12. San Francisco: Jossey-Bass, December 1981.

Financial Responsibility When Funds Expire. Most grant or contract funds do not last forever. Whether for training, research, demonstration, or service, grants and contracts are frequently used to increase organizational capacity in the program and human resources areas. Typically, the external resources are available for periods of one to three years. After that time, the organization is expected to assume the costs of operating the program. This is particularly true for demonstration projects whose purpose is to develop and test new ideas for adoption by others. Research grants and contracts have the greatest chance of being perpetuated, but significant achievements must be made in order to justify continued support for the same research concept. Service grants or contracts, usually made by state and local governments, are often continued, especially if the recipient is providing a quality level of service in a critical area and is highly supported by the community. Prior to applying for funds, serious consideration must be given as to the financial capacity of the organization to assume the costs of operating a program initially funded by external funds. Commitments to personnel hired must be spelled out clearly so that unrealistic expectations do not occur. It is often better to seek solid local support for a longer timespan than to accept a one-shot grant. The latter only creates a short-term fantasy which disappears and leaves the organization no better off than before.

Reporting and Management Requirements. Government grants and contracts in particular have significant reporting, evaluation, and management requirements. If your organization is not prepared or is unwilling to deal with major amounts of paperwork, or is philosophically unable to comply with government directives on equal hiring, access for the handicapped, and other requirements, government-funded projects are likely not for you. It takes openness and a willingness to comply with necessary directives and reporting requirements. It also takes great patience to complete all the steps in the bureaucratic process and an understanding that in the end it is all worthwhile to the receiving organization. Size is likely to be the greatest factor here—generally, the larger the organization, the greater the capacity to specialize and manage complex and detailed reporting requirements.

Organizational Priorities. Acceptance of major external funding often can have the effect of diverting the organization from its initial mission. This phenomenon occurs gradually until staff or board members begin to question the direction the organization is taking. A result can be acceptance of the new direction or a fight to return to the original mission. In any case, care should be given to the meaning of each project for the future of the organization; it is best that open discussion occur prior to submitting a proposal or at least before the award is accepted. Reordering organizational priorities may be healthy for the type of services offered in the community, but funding continuity should be a major consideration in applying for external funds.

Risktaking. Almost all proposals are initially a gamble. There are exceptions, but generally most awards are given on the basis of some type of competition. There is little to assure prospective applicants that they have the winning edge prior to the funding agency's review. Even in the corporate and foundation sectors, grants are subject to the whims and prejudices of boards of directors and the applicant must often rely on extensive cultivation of agency personnel to create a positive response. The applicant must first be willing to invest human and material resources in developing and producing the proposal. In many cases, as much work can go into the background development of a three-page foundation proposal as can go into a thirty- to fifty-page government proposal. Secondly, the prospective applicant must be willing to engage in risktaking to the extent that the investment in preparing the proposal can be written off if the proposal is not funded. A creative organization recognizes these facts and frequently will plan to use rejected proposal ideas as the basis for proposals to other funding sources. In any case, willingness to invest in risktaking, in the same way that a business might put up *venture capital,* can have significant rewards both in encouraging the organization to define its priorities and objectives, and in multiplying the investment if the project is funded.

Overall, these considerations can be valuable in choosing to apply or not to apply for external funds. The extent of dependence on external money, the capacity to assume financial operation when the funds end, assuming the burden of reporting requirements, the potential for reordering of organizational priorities, and willingness to invest in risktaking, are all important criteria for deciding whether or not to seek external funds. The smaller the organization, the greater the likelihood that these considerations will have a significant effect on the future of the organization. Each institution must carefully weigh the advantages and benefits against the disadvantages and costs of preparing and accepting an award. These decisions are best dealt with at the policy-making level of the organization—the board of directors or the chief administrator.

Overview of a Process Approach

The term *process* means different things to different people. As used here, it refers to a systematic, step-by-step framework for developing a proposal. Since the most complex proposals are usually those submitted to the federal government, the model reflects the typical features usually found in these types of proposals. Proposals to state and local governments, and those to corporations or foundations, usually require less detail in writing, although the background work may be very similar to proposals to the federal government. The process for the development of proposals for *contracts* with government agencies is very similar to the grant development process, however, it does differ in specific ways which will be noted at appropriate places in this chapter. The reader is also referred to the chapter on *contracting*.

The process approach to grant development is illustrated in Figure 1 and involves understanding of four general phases:

The Concept Development Phase. It is in this phase that the idea for the proposal is formulated, refined, and accepted as necessary to the mission of the applicant organization and as applicable to the intent of the funding source. This is the most critical of all stages, for if the idea becomes weakened, distorted, or lacks creative vigor, all subsequent steps are likely to be unsuccessful.

The Writing Phase. This is the nitty-gritty phase where the full proposal must be turned out page by page, section by section. The selection criteria of the funding agency along with its rules and regulations must be adhered to and the goals and objectives made consistent with the purpose and legislative intent of the program. There is no substitute for hard, diligent work at this phase of proposal development.

The Funding Agency Review Phase. In this phase, the action shifts to the review processes of the funding agency. In federal and state proposals, this process can be quite time-consuming and complex. In corporate and foundation proposals, it can be very simple—review by the board of directors. It is here in the review process where the quality of the proposal is matched against the selection criteria of the funding agency. Proposals are usually ranked by some form of point score from highest to lowest. Given the amount of dollars available for that funding cycle, the highest rated proposals are taken first until the funds allocated are exhausted. Those proposals not funded are often of high quality, but the limits of funds prohibit their acceptance for that funding cycle. This suggests that resubmitting a similar proposal in a subsequent cycle might increase the probability of receiving funds.

The Operational Phase. Those fortunate enough to receive funding will become active in this phase. It is here that staff are hired, accounts are established, the work of the project commences as specified in the proposal (or as negotiated), progress reports are made, and evaluations are conducted. Creative project management can often develop spinoff proposals which add to the continuity of the project currently being funded. A good investment in project resources can also go a long way toward maximizing new funding opportunities from a variety of funding sources.

The remainder of this chapter will discuss in detail each of the four phases.

Concept Development Phase

Two avenues of approach are available in the process of developing the project concept. The first is the assessment of needs, usually in terms of

Figure 1. Process of Developing and Obtaining Grants

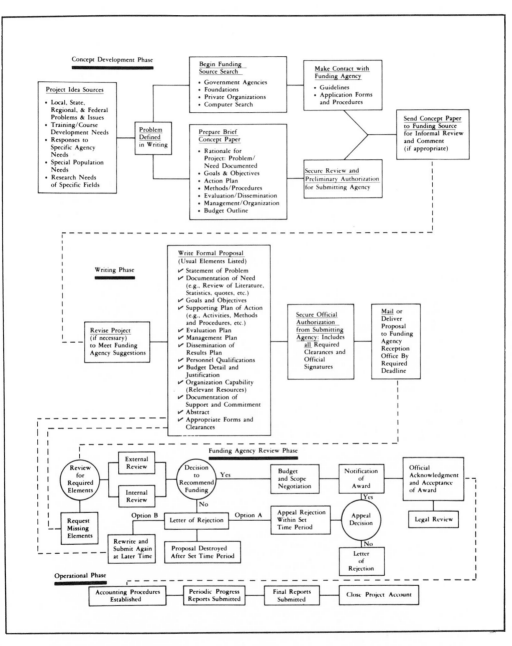

Source: Developed by Richard G. Maybee, 1979; appeared in Bonnie Brown, "Spotlight Interview: Meet Talented Grants Specialist Richard Maybee." *Funding Review*. Oct/Dec. 1980, *1* (1), 11.

the population to be served. This may include training of staff, developing new programs to meet a special need, serving the population, and/or improving organizational efficiency and operations. From these needs, specific project ideas are developed which help solve the problems or needs. The second avenue of approach starts with an examination of the selection criteria and the intent of potential funding sources. Based on the criteria, specific goals can be established which meet the needs of both the funding agency and the applicant organization. Matches and mismatches become evident at this point when information from needs assessment is compared with funding agency priorities. Attempts to match applicant needs with inappropriate funding agency programs and priorities usually result in rejected proposals. Thus, when used together, the two approaches should aid in identifying the most realistic and probable matches of project concepts with funding program sources.

Several areas of needs are often overlooked by many potential applicants. The first involves going beyond the applicant organization itself. Many opportunities exist for collaboration with other agencies, especially at local and regional levels. Occasionally, joint efforts with national level organizations can be highly rewarding. Private agency cooperation with public institutions is often distinctive and can offer valuable funding opportunities. A second area is the use of research projects as a form of evaluation of program or agency impact, needs assessment, or pilot testing of new approaches or programs. Often research projects can accomplish more than simply gathering data and their analysis. Local colleges and universities as well as qualified research and development organizations are the most likely sources of research collaboration. A third area, particularly important for continuing education organizations, is the development of periodic audits of corporate training needs. An example of this approach is used in Greensboro, North Carolina, where a consortium of local colleges does a periodic audit of the employee development and training needs of business and industrial firms in the area. Continuing education programs and other services are then developed to meet the identified needs, and these programs and services become the basis for grants or contracts from corporations, foundations, or the government.

Following initial verbal discussion of the project concept, it is a good idea to define in writing exactly the nature of the problem or need. This will allow others to assist in the confirmation of the origin of the need. Needs are often confused with wants (things that would be nice to have). Simply, a need is a description of a condition where problems or inadequacies are present; sometimes need is defined as the difference between "what is" and "what is necessary." The basis or criteria for making the judgment that a need exists should also be part of the need statement.

A further extension of the description of the problem is the development of a *concept paper*. A concept paper is usually from one to two pages in length. Elements normally found in a concept paper include: (1) a brief statement of the need or problem; (2) a statement of the proposed solution and its rationale; and (3) organizational management and capability to carry out the project. If space allows, mention of the major goals and objectives, along with evaluation and dissemination approaches can be included. A budget total should be included with the major categories distinguished, that is, personnel, equipment, and operations.

The concept paper has several important uses. First, it provides the project developer with an opportunity to organize concisely the project concept. Without this, the concept can remain vague and undefined. Writing things out has a clarifying influence on ideas. Second, the concept paper can be used to solicit peer feedback among one's colleagues. This is especially important at larger institutions where support must be present from a variety of organizational units in order for the project to function effectively. Third, the concept paper can be used to obtain an informal review or comment from the staff of the potential funding agency. Some agencies encourage this practice, especially the larger private foundations. Fourth, the concept paper can be employed as an abstract of the proposal when soliciting letters of support and commitment. Supporting agencies like to know specifically what they are getting involved in and it is a basic courtesy to provide them with that information in writing. It is highly recommended that personal contact be made with prospective supporting or participating agencies early in the project development period, followed promptly with the concept paper and a list of the questions to be responded to in the support letter. If specific commitments are being made, their financial value should be stated in the letter. Failure to begin this process early can result in loss of credibility and poor public relations.

As soon as the project is generally defined in writing, the search for appropriate funding sources should begin. Even if one or more are obvious, it is a good idea to do a more extensive search, especially of the private foundations and corporations. The more alternatives to choose from, the greater the likelihood that a source will be found.

Once the funding sources have been identified, careful research must be done to discover agency eligibility (type and geographical), the amount of typical awards, and the specifics of making an application. Direct contact with the funding agency is a requirement at this point. Valuable current information can be obtained by talking with a program officer or agency administrator. Most desirable is the discovery of implied selection criteria which may not be in writing. At the very least, forms and application materials must be requested.

Concomitant with contacting the funding agency, encouragement and authorization to continue proposal development should be sought from the policy-making board or individual of the applicant organization. All too often, proposal writers bypass this step and find after much hard work that the idea is rejected because it does not meet the priorities of the parent organization for that time period. Considerable disappointment can be avoided by good communication with superiors and policy makers regarding proposed concepts.

The concept development phase is primarily relevant to seeking grants rather than contracts because contracting agencies publish detailed specifications called Requests For Proposals (RFPs), which describe the project in terms of specific tasks to be performed. The writer's task, therefore, is to prepare a proposal which describes how that particular set of tasks will be accomplished. Thus, the grant development steps of defining the problem, preparing a concept paper, searching for funding sources, and informal review of concept papers are elements not common to the contracting process. It is important, however, to acquire copies of the request for proposal as quickly as possible and to secure organizational approval to pursue the contract.

Writing Phase

It is at this stage that comments and feedback are gathered from colleagues, funding agency staff, and others. Certain policy issues should be resolved regarding staff assignments, budget, and project activities. The revision of the project concept must be essentially complete before writing of the full proposal can begin.

The formal grant proposal generally takes two forms, depending on whether it is submitted to a government funding source or a private source. The most elaborate and complex proposals are those sent to the government. They require special budget forms, face sheets, and assurances to be completed and signed. Each funding agency and program category can have its own proposal organization and format, with research proposals differing considerably from other types of proposals. Typical of a program proposal are the following required items:

1. *An abstract* usually states why the funds are needed, what the funds will be spent on, and the capability of the organization to carry out the intended work.

2. *A statement of need* is usually keyed to the goals of the project and the intent of the funding agency. Consistency between needs identified and goals and objectives is crucial.

3. *Goals and objectives* specify the outcomes desired and the methods of obtaining them, often presented in outline form.

4. *Plan of action or program narrative* provides the rationale for the goals and objectives, discusses the philosophical approach for the project, and indicates specifics about the objectives and activities which are planned.

5. *Management plan* includes a time-line of activities often organized by objectives, includes staff responsibilities and organization schematic, and frequently includes roles and relationships of cooperating agencies in the project.

6. *Evaluation plan* describes objective by objective the various formative and summative methods of evaluating project outcomes. A chart showing objectives, outcomes, and positive or negative discrepancies can be included as a method of organizing the evaluation.

7. *Dissemination plan* when appropriate; a detailed plan showing how the project's constituency, parent organization, and significant other persons or organizations will be informed about both ongoing project activities and final project results.

8. *Organizational capability* portrays the physical, material, and human resources available to support the project. Brief resumes are appropriate in this section.

9. *Supporting agency documentation* provides evidence, usually in letter form, of support and commitments from cooperating agencies.

10. *Assurances and clearances* include signed assurances of compliance with funding agency requirements and clearances from local authorities that institutional rules have been met.

Proposals to private foundations, corporations, and other non-government entities usually require a short proposal of two or three pages. These proposals can be a refined concept paper and at the least should include: (1) a brief discussion of the problem or need with essential documentation; (2) the objectives of the project with the activities highlighted in a concise manner so that the budget items are obvious; (3) a statement indicating organizational capability to manage the funds and conduct the project, including brief mentions of the key project staff; and (4) a budget with specific lines for personnel, equipment, supplies, and other operating costs.

The narrative format for contract proposals will be specified in the RFP. There usually will be less emphasis on needs statements and goals and objectives, and greater emphasis on how specific tasks will be performed.

When the formal proposal has been written, it should be carefully and thoroughly proofread for spelling, grammar, and consistency of style. Official authorization must be obtained at required levels within the submitting organization. Signatures of organizational officials duly empowered to act on behalf of the organization's policy board must be affixed to appropriate forms or presented on cover letters.

Mailing and delivery of the proposal is a critical action that should not be taken for granted. Generally, there are two types of deadlines for submission of proposals. The first involves having the proposal delivered by a specified date and time. Failure to meet the time will almost always result in automatic rejection of the application. The second involves mailing the proposal by a specified date and usually includes the requirement that an official U.S. Postal Service date stamp be affixed on the mailing wrapper. Often these two types of deadlines are combined with the mailing deadline five or six days ahead of the hand delivery deadline. The use of private courier or delivery services becomes more risky the closer the deadline. National reputation is an important criteria for selection of a private courier service.

Funding Agency Review Phase

Review processes differ among funding agencies, particularly between government and private sectors. Generally, most government grants which are awarded on a competitive basis are reviewed by both funding agency staff and some type of external review panel. The agency program staff conducts an initial review to screen the proposals for applicant eligibility, inclusion of required forms, and proposal completeness. Where missing elements are noted, applicants are sometimes informed and given the opportunity to complete the application. This is not always done due to the large number of applications. Thus, all the more reason to check the proposal carefully before mailing.

Typically, the funding agency submits the proposals to qualified external reviewers either at their home location or at regional or national sites such as Washington, D.C. These reviewers rate the various sections of the proposal against the selection criteria which also include cost effectiveness and applicant capability. Often, after several rounds of discussions, the proposals are ranked according to total scores. The program staff of the agency then has the prerogative of revising these ratings, given knowledge of past applicant performance, geographical distribution, or other factors. Most often, the rankings of the review committee hold up fairly well into the assignment of funds.

If an application is rejected, an appeal procedure is normally available. This procedure, however, is used infrequently, as review panels and staff are typically very fair. Credibility of the applicant can sometimes be endangered within the appeal procedure.

Negotiation, conducted by one of the funding agency's grant or contract officers, usually occurs prior to official notification of award. It is important to remember that cuts in the proposal budget should have corresponding cuts in the scope of work of the project, otherwise the applicant implies that they were overbudgeted in the first place. Any attempt to do the same amount of work for less money will have negative effects on the staff and on future project proposals. Be prepared to respond to negotiations promptly and with the understanding of what can and cannot be cut to accomplish the purpose of the project. The applicant must usually respond in writing with the authorizing official's signature. Although the funding agency is not bound to follow through with funding, it usually does so after negotiation.

When project directors begin developing a proposal, they also set in motion a process that eventually will involve three other actors who have particular roles and expertise relating to the project. As shown in Figure 2, the first actor is the applicant organization's *project director* who initiates and develops the proposal. The second person is the *business manager* of the applicant organization, who commonly reviews outgoing proposals and will be involved in fiscal management of the funded project, and the third is the *program officer* at the funding agency, who is responsible for the content, program, or technical aspects of the proposal, and oversees the agency's evaluation of the proposal. Should the project be funded, the fourth actor is the funding agency's *contract or grant officer* who officially negotiates and authorizes the award and is responsible for approving any financial or legal changes in the project after it commences. This person has substantial authority and is, in fact, the only person who can legally

Figure 2. Roles and Relationships in Proposal Processing, Award Negotiations, and Project Management

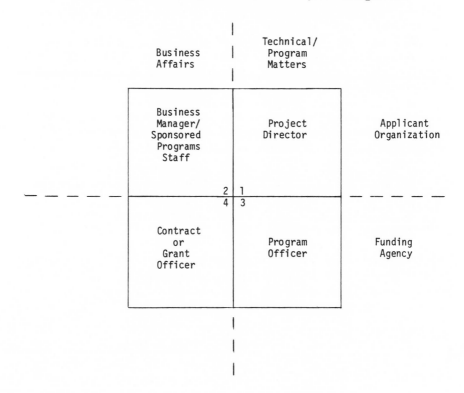

authorize changes in the contract or grant. Such changes should always be in writing. During negotiations it is very desirable to involve all four parties in the process, for they or their replacements will be involved for the life of the project and it is important that they are all conversant with the original agreement (Buskey, 1981).

Official notification by the funding agency constitutes an offer to accept the award. The receiving agency must officially accept the offer for the agreement to be binding. A legal review may be desirable or required before official acceptance.

With nongovernment funding sources, the review procedures are usually quite simple. The staff of the funding organization, or one of the board members, reviews the proposal and makes a recommendation to the full board. The board debates the merits of the proposal and makes the final decision, given all other proposals submitted. It is here that prior cultivation or previous awards can have an influence on the attitude and decision by the board. Adequate communications with program staff of the funding organization can reduce the likelihood of unexpected rejections.

The review process for contract proposals is different in two primary ways from that for grant proposals. First, contracts are reviewed internally rather than externally because the government is procuring a service or a product for its own use. Second, typically only one contract is awarded for a specific advertisement, and the government is seeking the best purchase for the least money. Thus, cost effectiveness is a more important consideration than in grant proposals.

Operational Phase

The project director for either grants or contracts assumes primary responsibility for the conduct of the project in the operational phase. The director must establish procedures to maintain accurate financial records of project expenses (both direct and contributed costs), submit periodic progress reports as required, supervise the activities of project staff, and submit interim and final reports. A well-thought-out evaluation process will do much to contribute to progress reporting and will develop the information to be used in the final, summative report.

A good project director recognizes the need to invest small amounts of project resources in identifying new funding sources and/or developing subsequent proposals. This type of investment should begin at least midway through the total project period. Often, at least a year's lead time is required for development, submission, and review.

Time Allocation for Proposal Development

Figure 3 suggests very simply that about two thirds of the time involved in proposal development is in background activities. Creating the

Figure 3. Pie Diagram of Time Use for Proposal Development

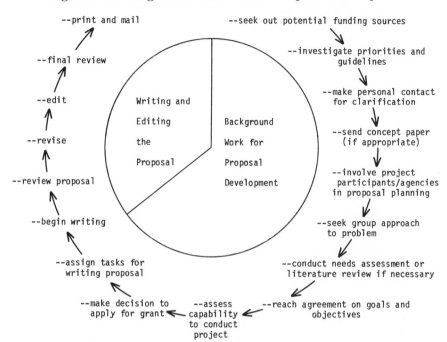

concept, investigating the potential funding agencies, seeking organizational or community support, and conducting needs assessments are all likely to be quite time-consuming. Only about a third of the time is actually consumed in writing and editing the proposal. A major fault of most inexperienced proposal writers is that they begin writing before they complete the background work. This is frequently counterproductive and may require major rewriting of sections of the proposal.

Summary

The process approach suggests an orderly recognition of major activities necessary to complete the development of a proposal, especially those submitted to government funding agencies. Shortcuts are possible, but may backfire later in the process. Understanding of concept development, writing, review, and operational phases as a total system should help prospective applicants prepare themselves for developing successful projects.

Reference

Buskey, J. H. "The Proposal Process." Paper presented at Proposal Writing Institute, Virginia Polytechnic Institute and State University, Blacksburg, Va., January 15, 1981.

Richard G. Maybee is director of government, corporate, and foundation relations at Guilford College in Greensboro, North Carolina. He has conducted numerous workshops and seminars on proposal writing and grant development and is a trainer for the National Grant Development Institute of Pocatello, Idaho.

*As budgets tighten, the choice of whether or not to
seek external resources may no longer be there. For
many continuing education programs, external
resources may mean the difference between a strong
program or mere survival. Administrators who
organize for efficient proposal development will be
the ones with strong continuing education programs.*

Organizing for Efficient Proposal Writing

Frank G. Adams

Proposal writing is not the major responsibility of most continuing education administrators. Indeed, the proposals written by the administrator
may be only those that are routine renewals or continuation applications.
Venturing into new areas of proposal writing becomes time-consuming
and disorganizing if the administrator is assuming that proposals are "just
something we do in the office."

The administrator may be quite capable of identifying funding
sources and receiving requests for proposals (RFPs) from dozens of agencies, but unless proposals are dealt with through an organized and efficient
process the results may be negative. The administrator, after spending
hours attempting to meet deadlines, responding to a variety of priorities,
and trying to track the flow of the proposal through the organization, may
then return to the less risky proposals in despair and frustration.

Organizing for efficient proposal writing is not a difficult task, but
it does take a few weeks of intra-institutional discussions and solid commitment to the process by the organization and its senior officers. A few
simple steps can be followed that will facilitate the process and increase the
number of proposals submitted, and most likely, the number of awards
received.

J. Buskey (Ed.). *New Directions for Continuing Education: Attracting External Funds
for Continuing Education,* no. 12. San Francisco: Jossey-Bass, December 1981.

Step One: The Mission Statement

The mission statement is a clear, concise declaration of the precise mission of the continuing education office. It defines the mission of the institution and the basic goals for continuing education at the institution.

Why Is a Mission Statement So Vital? As the administrator becomes more proficient in securing external resources, opportunities will seem unlimited. The administrator can easily get caught up in the process of getting proposals funded without analyzing the implications or the impact of the funds on the institution or the continuing education program. In other words, external funding becomes the objective rather than the means for achieving the objective.

A few years ago, a midwestern university found itself delivering hot meals to senior citizens. The university president and the board of trustees debated for weeks with the adminstrator in charge of the catering grant as to how this program related to higher education. On another occasion, an adult education administrator secured funds in such proportions that the adult program became larger than all other programs in the school district. This became quite an issue when the board of trustees could not provide similar programs for high school students. In both situations, the continuing education administrators did not have a clear and definitive mission statement that clearly defined the role of continuing education in these organizations.

External resources should be sought to help meet a locally identified need that is clearly within the scope of the institution. Once the mission statement is drafted and approved by the appropriate authorities, including possibly the governing board, the administrator is in a position to seek external funds that will assist the institution in carrying out its mission.

Drafting a Mission Statement. The mission statement, although a one-page document, identifies the characteristics of the institution that define its role within its geographical service area. In other words, why does the institution exist and what are the parameters that govern its existence?

Along with the mission statement are the broad goals the institution attempts to achieve within the confines of its physical, human, and financial resources. One of the institution's goal statements should address the purpose of continuing education within the institution. The function of continuing education is then seen as a major goal of the mission and provides a legitimate base for continuing education objectives and programming.

Objectives may be established annually or every few years, depending upon the dynamics of the community served. The administrator may even wish to set annual objectives in priority order so that staff efforts may be adjusted accordingly during the year. One of the objectives may be to seek outside resources to assist in meeting other objectives.

The mission statement, including goals and objectives, creates a broad framework to support the continuing education effort. It acts to provide focus, continuity, and credibility to the programs offered. Additionally, it sets the boundaries for what proposals and programs will be developed to achieve specific objectives. A mission statement has little validity or use if the governing board or chief executive officer has not formally given approval to the document.

Step Two: Organizing Information

When the administrator first begins a search for funds, only a few sources may seem appropriate. Within a short while, however, the possibilities appear infinite. The federal government alone provides hundreds of opportunities. National and regional foundations provide several hundred more; and corporations, when approached properly, can provide many additional opportunities. How to keep track of possible funding sources seems like a full-time job. This need not be. With an appropriate, limiting process, the administrator can narrow the number of possible sources to one or two hundred of which seventy-five to ninety will truly be possibilities. Defining and limiting sources is an important activity.

The limiting process creates an information system through which a large amount of information about potential sources flows to the administrator but only the most viable possibilities are retained. In this way, the administrator maintains an active file of possibilities that relate to the organization's objectives. From these, enough proposals can be developed to increase financial support by hundreds of thousands of dollars. Yet, the administrator has not become a full-time grantsperson.

The Information System

At this point the administrator who has not actively developed proposals should be wary of a desire to acquire information. Commercial publications and government documents can inundate the administrator with information, most of which is not manageable at this point. Many administrators, however, will still tend to plunge right into acquiring documents, publications, personal contacts, computerized listings, and other data. The quest for "where the money is" tends to be overwhelming. Too much information leading to too many opportunities with strict submission deadlines may be more than an already busy administrator can handle.

Developing a Card File. Using a three-by-five-inch card, the administrator can record the essential information necessary to keep track of funding sources. The file should contain a card for each potential funding source. Reviewing current grants and contracts in operation will provide a start. From there the *Catalog of Federal Domestic Assistance* (U.S. Office of Management and Budget, 1980) will give the administrator information on every possible federal grant funding program. There are so many sources here that culling is very important. Selecting programs that appear to match the institution's mission statement on continuing education is vital. Next, a review of the *Foundation Directory* (1979) will not only lead to identification of foundations throughout the nation, but will also help identify those foundations that are willing to support the programs the continuing education administrator wishes to develop.

The resource index should indicate the name, address, and telephone number of the funding source; the contact person; the average dollar amount awarded; and the areas or priorities eligible for awards. Once completed, the file can be added to as new sources are identified through professional journals, conferences, and personal contacts. It should be kept current and contain only those sources clearly related to the objectives of the office.

Using Contact Follow-Up. One of the most devastating experiences the administrator can have is to contact a possible funding source only to discover that other members of the same organization have recently made a similar contact. An important rule to follow is to always maintain a record of contacts. In some offices each funding agency listed in the index file has a folder in which staff members can leave memoranda concerning contacts made with the agency. Some use a notebook readily accessible to the staff to add information. Other offices designate one person to be the contact person for the office. At any rate, the administrator needs to control who contacts the agency and for what purpose. Otherwise, the continuing education administrator or the fund-seeking office may appear to the funding agency as unorganized or inept.

This is a particularly difficult problem in large organizations, and some large universities have established both development offices and sponsored research offices to facilitate the contact and solicitation process. It is always a good idea to find out what processes your institution employs and then use them to your advantage.

Information Gathering. Being able to secure the right information at the right time and appropriately pursuing the funding agency is an essential part of proposal writing activity. The administrator can do very little to respond effectively to proposal guidelines if the information arrives only one or two days before the deadline.

Step Three: Developing Standard Components
in the Programming Narrative

Over ninety percent of the grants awarded for programs, whether for curriculum development, demonstrations, or continuing education, require the same basic information. Knowing this, efficiency is enhanced by standardizing those components that are common to most proposals. In this way, the administrator does not have to repeat the process completely each time a proposal is written. Some of the components which can be standardized are needs assessments, institution identity, institution location, institution capability, organizational structure diagrams, personnel position descriptions, maps of the institution's service areas, standard signature sheets, timetables, and government assurance forms.

One of the essential aspects of standardization begins with selecting one typewriter to be used for all proposals. Especially desirable is a typewriter with memory capacity and the ability to change type styles quickly. Those components which have been drafted as standard elements will have the same type as the body of the document. Through standardization of common components, the administrator can save a good deal of time and effort. The time and effort saved can be used to initiate new proposals. Through standardization of components, administrators who previously completed four or five proposals annually find they can produce twenty to thirty proposals in the same time. Although what can be standardized does depend upon local institutional requirements as well as government regulations, some standardization is always possible.

Signature Page. Although most government agencies require signatures on official forms, many institutions require that a signature page be inserted which clarifies through the signatures who has reviewed the proposal. In most cases, the same officers review all proposals. Therefore, a signature page already complete and ready for signatures can save much time and assure that appropriate officers have reviewed the proposal.

Needs Assessment. Continuing education administrators sometimes carry out a needs assessment for each proposal. This activity is mostly redundant and often unnecessary. If a mission statement has been developed, the administrator then decides what process is to be used to specify the needs to be met and conducts a needs assessment. The result may be a rather lengthy report which can be summarized in six to ten pages with one additional page that specifies how the proposal will meet one or more of the identified needs. In this way, instead of conducting a lengthy needs assessment for each proposal, the administrator drafts a few paragraphs relating the need to be met by the proposal to an overall needs assessment.

The proposal thus demonstrates that a comprehensive assessment has been done and shows how the administrator intends to meet one or more of the needs through the project being proposed. Competence is demonstrated to the funding agency by giving the agency a clear description of how the proposal is a part of a clearly identified needs analysis and an overall institutional plan.

Institutional Identity and Capability. Most funding agencies require a description of the fund-seeking institution—where it is, what its purpose is, and how capable it is of carrying out externally funded programs. Once this has been stated, there is no need to rewrite this component for each new proposal. One well-written statement addressing identity and capability should suffice and can be routinely inserted in each proposal.

Organizational Structure. Most continuing education offices have an organizational chart that names the basic units of the permanent organization and shows their relationships to each other. Sometimes externally funded new projects become part of an existing unit, and other times they may be set up as a separate unit. A standard organizational chart (or charts) on which the titles or names of project personnel or project units may be inserted can eliminate the need for redrafting the organization chart for each proposal and can save hours of effort for the administrator and the office staff. Chapter Four contains an example of an organization chart.

Personnel Descriptions. In continuing education projects, three position descriptions seem to be used consistently. These are the project manager, the clerical staff, and the instructors. In each case, regardless of institutional titles, the positions and functions tend to be the same. Clerical staff at an institution have similar duties. Project managers, whether titled project coordinator, director, or supervisor, tend to have the same functions. The same is true of instructors. An analysis of these similarities can result in a common description for all personnel working on projects funded from external resources. Once drafted, these descriptions can be inserted into each proposal rather than rewritten. Standardizing position descriptions will cut down on time and effort by 20 to 30 percent.

There is an additional advantage to this element. Since most institutional policies and government regulations require equity in job positions, standardization insures that project personnel have equitable job descriptions. Salary determinations, work load equity, title and status equity are also accounted for in this way. Not only has the administrator saved time and effort in producing the proposal, but also potential personnel problems may have been eliminated, especially as the number of funded projects increases.

Timetables. A major problem of proposals is the timetable. Many administrators try to identify by month and day the time for completion of activities or objectives. If the funding agency is unable to award the contract or grant on the schedule proposed, the administrator may then have to revise the entire timetable. Generally, projects are awarded for one year and objectives are expected to be completed within that time frame. By devising a standard time chart identifying months by the first month of the project rather than the calendar month, it becomes easy to project time lapses on the chart. Thus, what ordinarily takes hours to project and to graph now takes only a few moments. Chapter Four contains an example of a time chart.

Diagramming Proposal Activities. A key component of an efficient proposal writing system is the ability to graphically demonstrate what the objectives and activities will do. The continuing education administrator will tend to draft programmatic proposals. That is, the proposal is designed to provide some learning activity or service to participants in the program. Although the objectives are quite clear to the administrator, the funding agency staff may still have some initial difficulty understanding what will happen to the participants in the project.

It is very important to develop a flow chart or diagram that illustrates what will happen to the participants. As the diagram is used in several proposals, the administrator may find that, although the content of a project changes, the flow of participants through a project's activities is essentially the same. One or two common flow charts will emerge. The chart itself can be developed with labels that change to identify the chart with a particular project. Thus, another very vital part of the proposal becomes a routine function.

Continuing education administrators who actively pursue external funding may find that several other components of the proposals can be made routine. If the administrator can keep in mind that the objectives, the procedures for meeting the objectives, and the evaluation plan are the basic framework around which all other components of the proposal are fitted, then standardization will save time and effort, and create an efficient proposal writing mechanism.

Step Four: Developing Standard Components in the Budget

Probably the most difficult phase of developing an effective proposal is budgeting. Here the administrator must balance the funding agency's guidelines and funds with the institution's standard budgeting process. Common elements of the budget are often left out by oversight or the inability of the administrator to keep the minute details of possible budget items in mind.

Here, standardization is not a method for providing easily inserted documents into the proposal, but rather a reminder of those elements which might be included. Again, the administrator need not research costs each time a new proposal is developed. An administrator can reduce time and control the budget so that it fits the institution's budget process.

A review of inhouse salary and fringe benefit policies is a must. The implications of these policies need to be articulated in the proposal budget. In other words, the proposal budget should reflect institutional budgeting policies as well as the funding agency's parameters. One sure way to accomplish this is to draft a comprehensive mock budget that can be used as a guide. It will not help to determine actual dollar amounts but it will be a reminder to review certain items. Once the institution and funding agency have approved the proposal, the budget becomes an almost fixed document with little room to juggle funds.

There is no more time-consuming problem than to discover that while the project secretary is on vacation, the project failed to provide for a substitute. Another common problem is providing for mailings of thousands of brochures or newsletters but failing to budget postage.

A mock budget drafted to cover as many line item costs as possible becomes a handy checklist against which to compare actual proposal budgets.

Summary

The main body of a proposal consists of the program narrative and the budget. The key features of the program narrative are objectives, activities, and evaluation. The remainder of the application tends to be the justification for the project, clarification of how the project operates, and descriptions of the institution and its capabilities. Through standardization of the components of these elements, the administrator is able to be more productive and more efficient. Additionally, more time can be spent on the essentials of the program narrative. In most evaluation criteria, the program agency places high priority on the quality of objectives, procedures for carrying out these objectives, and how the project is evaluated. It is important to spend the time available on these important items and routinize as many other elements as possible. Quite possibly those who avoid the proposal writing experience, or who have had a bad experience, were not organized to handle the proposal; the process of developing the document became time consuming or they did not have the right funding source identified. More than likely they had no systematic approach for identifying and developing a proposal.

As institutional budgets become tighter and as greater numbers of adults return to school through continuing education programs, the grant and contract process will become one of the key methods for continuing education administrators to increase their budgets. Those who develop an efficient development process are likely to be the ones who end up with a fair share of the available external funds.

References

The Foundation Directory. (Seventh Edition.) New York: The Foundation Center, 1979.

U.S. Office of Management and Budget. Catalog of Federal Domestic Assistance. Washington, D.C.: U.S. Government Printing Office, 1980.

Frank G. Adams is dean of open campus at the College of Lake County and is President of Educational Resources Institute. In the past five years, he has been involved in raising more than ten million dollars for continuing education programs for the college. Additionally, he conducts grants and contracts seminars through the Bureau of Business and Technology, New York.

*Private philanthropy will not come close to taking up
the slack produced by federal budget cuts . . .*

Funding Sources:
How to Find Out
Where the Money Is

Twila C. Liggett

Almost overnight—with the consolidation of federally funded programs
into block grants imminent—the challenge of identifying funding sources
has increased exponentially. Of the three major categories of available
funds, federal resources have been one of the largest. A major change in
government funding will affect the other major types of sources—
foundations and corporations—and create temporary instability. Searching for funds, never an easy task, will require more ingenuity, creativity and
persistence than ever before.

Funding Trends—Shifting Ground

There has always been a close relationship between governmental,
corporate, and foundation funding in the sense that funds received from
one entity frequently helped to generate or were used to match funds from
another. Consequently, when one source is altered or eliminated, the
balance suffers.

While funding trends could be better predicted by a soothsayer, most
knowledgeable sources foresee an era of grant funds controlled by state and

J. Buskey (Ed.). *New Directions for Continuing Education: Attracting External Funds
for Continuing Education,* no. 12. San Francisco: Jossey-Bass, December 1981.

local government entities. And, as the *Grantsmanship Center News* recently editorialized, this is unfortunate since "(s)tate and local jurisdictions have proved woefully ill-equipped to handle the technical, management, and program demands of contemporary problems" ("The Bucks. . . ," 1981, p. 92).

Originally, the Reagan administration claimed that where funding was cut or eliminated, philanthropic organizations would compensate for federal reductions. In actuality, "private philanthropy will not come close to taking up the slack produced by federal budget cuts . . ." according to a study conducted by the Urban Institute (*Federal Grants and Contracts Weekly*, 1981, p. 1).

The best advice for continuing education administrators in search of funds is to track the legislative process and to develop or maintain a systematic approach to the funding search. To that end, the remainder of this chapter provides an overview of traditional as well as computer-based resources, outlines elements of a systematic search, and touches on some examples of continuing education funding sources. This article is not exhaustive and the reader is urged to explore further for specific funding needs.

Major Types of Funding Sources

Funding sources usually fall into three major groups: government, foundation and corporate. Given the changes underway in Washington, a discussion of federal government resources may be an historical one; however, the Congressional budgetary process involves a great deal of compromise and can be exceedingly lengthy. Thus, a grasp of what now exists will help the astute administrator keep track of the final outcome.

Government Sources. Government funds have always been available at three levels: federal, state and local. At most local levels, grant funds are earmarked for very specific programs and, if made available through a grant proposal process, are for very small amounts. At the state level, a variety of funds have been available but, in many cases, qualified applicants were restricted to state, county or local governmental entities or agencies. Corrections, Comprehensive Employment and Training Act (CETA), welfare, health, and education are a few examples of state agencies or programs which have provided small grant programs at the state level.

The money-funneling details for block grants have not as yet been determined but logic would indicate that state governments will become the most important dispersion points for the block grants. Hence, the development of contacts with the appropriate state agency or agencies prior to actual disbursement of funds would seem to be of prime concern to those seeking such funds.

Unfortunately, the type of aggregate amounts available from federal grants will diminish considerably. To illustrate, consider the following scenario. In the past, federal program XYZ has been awarding $2.5 million in grants with an average grant amount of $250,000. After budget cuts of around 20 percent, the remaining money is disbursed through block grants to 50 states. *If* a state targets that particular program for funding, the amount available at the state level could conceivably total $30,000 to $40,000, depending upon how administrative costs in the state level are calculated. In turn, *if* that state elicits proposals, it is possible that individual grants might range from $5,000 to $10,000. If forty-nine other states follow suit, the result is that the money is divided among more people, but to what avail?

Locating government funds may require creative solutions such as consortia or other cooperative arrangements in order to acquire sufficient levels of funding necessary to support ongoing or new projects. This will not suffice for many projects, however, and, while competition will be fierce, efforts to obtain foundation and corporate funding will have to be increased.

Foundations. Kurzig defines a foundation as ". . . a nongovernmental, nonprofit organization with funds and programs managed by its own trustees or directors and established to maintain or aid social, educational, charitable, religious, or other activities serving the common welfare, mainly through the making of grants" (1980, p. 3).

There are five major types of foundations: national or general purpose, special purpose, company or corporate sponsored, community, and family. National or general foundations, which include most of the large ones, such as the Ford or Carnegie foundations, award funds to projects which are primarily national in scope. Special purpose foundations fund a special interest such as medicine, business education, farming or other very specific concern. Corporate foundations usually fund programs of local interest and impact. Federal law allows companies to contribute up to 10 percent of their income (although 2 percent is the average) to educational or charitable causes. With a few exceptions, these funds are available in the immediate area where the company has plants or offices. Community foundations are frequently broad in scope; however, their funds are usually distributed within a limited area. The Cleveland Foundation, for example, is one of the largest community foundations. Family foundations are usually small and controlled by a donor or a donor's family; family foundation funding is very selective and determined by that family's specific interests ("Developing Successful Proposals . . . ," 1979).

Major resources for identifying the appropriate foundations for a proposed program or project are discussed below. Needless to say, a thorough and systematic research plan is essential to identify possible sources and to eliminate inappropriate foundations.

Corporations. "The first and foremost law of corporate giving is that virtually all donations are made in the self-interest of the corporation and/or its decision-makers" (Hillman, 1980, p. 3). When approaching a private corporation, remember that while they may have a systematic giving plan, this can range from $1000 a year for the local heart fund drive to some very significant contributions, such as construction funds for renovation or an addition to the continuing education center. While contacts are important in any of the funding categories, developing personal relationships with decision-makers at a corporation are imperative when seeking funds directly from business and industry.

A Systematic Search—The Key

An essential first step to a systematic search is to define and describe clearly the need for funding and, if a grant proposal is envisioned, to develop a concise statement of the project idea or concept. Such a tool will give the means to define or sharpen the focus on viable funding sources. This is essential to the next step, that of researching specific foundations, federal programs or corporations for a *match*. While each step in the process always seems to take a very long time, vague generalizations and unfocused searching can be extremely costly in terms of staff time and, in some instances, will result in missing grant opportunities and proposal deadlines.

Besides the government, foundation and corporate resources described briefly below, there are literally hundreds of books, newsletters and articles which describe funding possibilities and approaches. Once familiar with primary sources, it would be helpful to check institutional and public libraries for specific trade or professional journals, special interest areas or paperback guides and newsletters which regularly report on funding sources. Some additional resources can be found in the references at the end of this chapter.

Government. Four major publications are available at the federal level: *The Federal Register, Commerce Business Daily,* the *Catalog of Federal Domestic Assistance* (CFDA), and *The United States Government Manual.* Federal agencies that fund grants, as opposed to contracts, publish their rules and regulations and their guidelines for grant applications in the *Federal Register.* It is one of the major documents announcing the availability of federal grants, and information on grant programs includes how to apply, deadlines, proposal evaluation criteria, applicable cost principles, and cost-sharing and matching requirements. The *Commerce Business Daily* lists every Request for Proposal, or RFP, that exceeds $5,000 from federal agencies that are offering contracts as opposed to grants. RFPs are listed under the "Services" section in sub-categories, for example, medical services, expert and consultant services, and training services. To obtain a complete RFP, a written request must be submitted to the contact person. The *Catalog of Federal Domestic Assistance* provides a comprehensive listing and description of federal programs and activities which have funding capabilities. "Information Contacts" listed for each program may be utilized to obtain additional information regarding funding potential and "Related Programs" refers to other similar projects in the *CFDA*. The *United States Government Manual*, the federal government's official handbook, provides additional background about each federal agency's requirements, activities, and key officials.

Foundations. A major resource for foundation information is the Foundation Center, which is a national service organization established and supported by foundations to provide a single authoritative source of information on foundation giving. The Center compiles descriptive data and statistics on the foundation field, serves as a resource for potential foundation grant applicants, and publishes numerous guides and reference books. A major resource of the Center is *The Foundation Center Source Book Profiles*, a monthly subscription service. The *Source Book* provides detailed, comprehensive funding pattern profiles of the 1,000 largest foundations described by subject area (for example, education), type of grant (for example, seed money, research), and type of recipient (for example, community college, symphony guild). Information about the Center services can be obtained by writing the New York office. Foundation Center information or data can also be obtained at one of their four national centers or in the regional centers or collections which are located at many major university and public libraries. Several computer data bases also include Foundation Center information.

Other major Foundation Center resources include *The Foundation Directory, The Foundation Grants Index, Foundation News: The Journal of Philanthropy,* and *Foundation Grants to Individuals.* The *Directory* provides addresses, names of officers, purposes, and financial resources of private foundations with assets exceeding $1,000,000 or annual grants totaling $100,000 or more. General background information includes area of giving, addresses, telephone numbers, current financial data, and grant application information. The *Grants Index* lists foundations which, during the prior year, awarded grants of $5,000 or more. The *News*, a bimonthly journal for foundation administrators, contains book reviews and articles which may have some interest for potential applicants. *Grants to Individuals* emphasizes grants and awards from approximately 950 foundations to individuals. Its most useful feature is a twelve-page introduction which includes an overview of funding agencies.

In recent years a number of state foundation directories have been published which attempt to list information about all the foundations in a specific state. *Funding Review* recently published an "Annotated List of State Foundation Directories" (1981).

Corporations. A primary factor in corporate philanthropy is the current financial status of the organization. Good profits can lead to a great deal of activity while a poor year may lead to a drastic reduction in philanthropic efforts. Because of this variability in funds and the fact that very few corporations have a formalized grant process, it is a rare company that has established guidelines. Some of the Foundation Center information may be helpful. Also available are some commercial publications such as *The Corporate Fund Raising Directory*. The best approach, however, is to make personal contact with the top management or company directors and convince them of your project's compatibility with company goals or of the project's benefits to the corporate image or employees. Corporations may prefer to donate volunteer services, equipment, or other materials instead of outright cash. For background information about corporations, the *Register of Corporations, Directors, and Executives* (Standard and Poor) or *Million Dollar Directory* and *Directory of Corporate Managements* (Dun and Bradstreet) can be found in most public libraries. A new publication of the Foundation Center, *Corporate Foundation Profiles*, should also be consulted.

Research. None of this information will be of much help, however, if the identification and research process is not a systematic one. As background information is obtained, through the use of print references or, more ideally, a computer search, existing funding sources must either be eliminated or included for in-depth investigation.

From initial sources, it should be possible to determine some or most of the following: program objectives or possible fundable topic areas, eligibility requirements, contact persons, uses and restrictions of the funds, and range of grant awards. Try to establish whether foundations, and occasionally government sources, have specific geographic limitations. For instance, the Northwest Area Foundation in Minnesota only funds projects in the western states where the Great Northern Railroad ran.

Once apparently compatible funding sources are identified, make contact by telephone or letter and request more information—such as an annual report, guidelines, or a guide to the grant application process.

At this point, the project idea should be expanded into a short concept paper which can provide the basis for further communication with the funding source. In some cases, the concept paper can be sent to the organization along with a request for a personal visit with a representative of the program to ascertain their initial interest in the idea.

While a scattergun approach has been used by many potential applicants (for example, a form letter is sent to 200 funding sources) this approach is almost always nonproductive. Whether a government agency, foundation or corporation, that entity usually has predetermined goals, objectives and a purpose for their available funds. It is much more efficient to zero in on the smaller number of organizations or federal programs that appear to match a specifically described need for funds.

Finally, follow up any and all contacts and keep an ongoing record of the responses. While some of the sources may not be appropriate for current needs, that could change in the future.

Computer-Based Searches—A Major Tool

Computer technology has revolutionized the funding-search process. The grant seeker might once have spent days and even months obtaining "hard" copy and scanning volumes of print information. In contrast, a well-planned computer search of thirty to forty minutes can not only identify appropriate sources, but can also refine and eliminate inappropriate ones.

Major Data Vendors. There are three major companies or vendors that provide computerized search services (Barkan and Slade, 1981): Lockheed Information Systems (LIS), also referred to as DIALOG; System Development Corporation Search Service (SDC), also referred to as ORBIT; and Bibliographic Retrieval Services, Inc. (BRS). These three companies provide bibliographical references to printed materials drawn from approximately 150 data bases on a wide range of topics including federal and foundation funding.

Three other vendors provide access to non-bibliographic data bases which are primarily oriented toward business and industry: DIALCOM, Inc., General Electric Information Services Company, and the Service Bureau Company.

It is possible to contact the vendors directly for further information (Barkan and Slade, 1981):

Bibliographic Retrieval Services, Inc. (BRS)
  702 Corporation Park
  Scotia, NY 12302
  (800) 833-4707
  Data base:
  Smithsonian Science Information Exchange

DIALCOM Inc.
  1104 Spring Street
  Silver Spring, MD 20910
  (301) 588-1572
  Data base:
  Federal Assistance Program Retrieval System (FAPRS)

General Electric Information Services Company
 1050 17th Street, N.W., Suite 850
 Washington, D.C. 20036
 (202) 467-6590
 Data base:
 Federal Assistance Program Retrieval System (FAPRS)

Lockheed Information Systems (LIS) DIALOG
 3460 Hillview Avenue
 Palo Alto, CA 94304
 (800) 227-1960 (outside California)
 (800) 982-5838 (in California)
 Data bases:
 Educational Resources Information Center (ERIC)
 Foundation Directory
 Foundation Grants Index
 National Foundations
 Smithsonian Science Information Exchange
 U.S. Department of Agriculture/Current Research Information System

SDC Search Service ORBIT
 2500 Colorado Avenue
 Santa Monica, CA 90406
 (800) 421-7229 (outside California)
 (800) 352-6689 (in California)
 Data bases:
 Smithsonian Science Information Exchange
 Grants Information System

The Service Bureau Company
 Time-Sharing Services
 500 West Putnam Avenue
 Greenwich, CT 06830
 Data base:
 Federal Assistance Program Retrieval System (FAPRS)

Computer Access and Utilization. Most university libraries and many large public libraries have access to one (usually DIALOG) or more of the computer services. It is not necessary to be a computer operator or even particularly knowledgeable about computers to use these services. A computer search staff member will utilize key words, topics, and other selection indicators to identify the appropriate source and conduct the search. In many instances, however, a searcher may not be familiar with grants or funding source information since the funding data bases are a small minority of the total number of data bases available on any given system. Therefore, be prepared to discuss in some detail precisely what you need in order to avoid costly mistakes once you are connected on-line to the computer service.

Costs are based on an hourly fee and vary according to the difficulty of the task and the pricing structure of the computer service company. Computer searches may cost as little as $5 to $10 or as much as $100. The search itself usually costs less than the printout; for example, at thirty cents per item, a listing of 100 entries can count up quickly. Records that are printed at the local terminal will cost considerably more than if the record is obtained from the company's main computer and mailed. The key to cost containment is a well-planned strategy, clearly defined need, and a skillful computer operator or searcher.

Sample Search. In order to illustrate the computer search process, a very limited search was conducted for foundation funding sources for continuing education. Key words used were *continuing education, adult education,* and *community education.* A brief overview of the search follows.

During an initial meeting with one of the library's computer search service staff, a search request questionnaire form was filled out. The form included requests for: a description of the nature of the search—*funding sources for adult and continuing education;* any limitations or exclusions—*awards between 1978 and 1980;* and a list of descriptors—*continuing education, adult education,* and *community education.* The *Foundation Grants Index* was then accessed through DIALOG (LIS).

Initially, the computer calculated the number of funded grants for each of the key words. With information available for over 300 awards in the adult education and community education categories, respectively, and 800 listings for 1980 community education, the search had to be narrowed. An additional limitation of grants for 1980 only was made and the community education category eliminated. Another computer calculation of listings revealed approximately 100 entries.

At this point, continuing education was dropped and the descriptor *lifelong learning* was added as a cross reference to adult education. The computer then reported six listings. For such a small listing, it was as cost effective to ask for a printout from the terminal as to have one mailed. Two examples of the computer entries are given below:

17/2/1
2170728
Haas (Evelyn and Walter), Jr., Fund, CA
   $7,000 to Fromm Institute for Lifelong Learning, Friends of, San Francisco, CA. For scholarship support for education program for people over fifty. 78
   KEY WORDS: Education (adult)/Learning

14/2/2
2140529
Kellogg (W.K.) Foundation, MI
$420,450 to Madonna College, Livonia, MI. To establish regional continuing education model to coordinate lifelong learning for adults in southeastern Michigan. 2/15/80
KEY WORDS: Education (adult)

While these entries contain information similar to that in the *Foundation Grants Index*, the fifteen minutes it took to obtain the listings was a fraction of the time required to search by hand. In addition, if the initial descriptions were compatible with an already identified funding need judgments could have been made as to whether to request additional information from, for example, the *Foundation Directory* or the *Foundation Center Source Book Profiles*. If the funding source, based on further details, looked promising, the administrator would be ready to move to the next step—contacting the funding source directly for specific guidelines and other relevant information.

Continuing Education—Where Are the Funds?

If the administrator is looking for just *any* funds, then utilizing the key words of *adult, continuing, and community education* in a computer search should yield a plethora of potential sources; however, vague and overgeneralized searches are largely unproductive and expensive in a computer search. To investigate and research a listing of 800 community education or 345 adult education awards is prohibitive in terms of time and expense. By clearly specifying areas of need, such as *lifelong learning,* or *counseling adults,* a much closer match and possibly a more appropriate funding organization, can be identified.

In the past, major funding has been available from categorical government programs in the arts and humanities, adult and continuing education, Title I of the Higher Education Act, and the Fund for the Improvement of Postsecondary Education (FIPSE)—to name a few. Large and small foundations have funded, and most likely will continue to fund, innovative projects in specific areas; however, the competition for these funds will increase as the federal block grants become a reality. The administrator must become creative and inventive.

Some administrators have already experimented with developing courses or specific programs in conjunction with a local corporation for that company's employees with the goal that some of the programs will be underwritten by that company for any interested student or for the general community.

Summary

There is no magic formula for locating funds. Systematic investigation and research methods are mandatory for the successful administrator. Utilization of computer technology and the development and maintenance of personal contacts in funding organizations can also facilitate the targeting of appropriate funding sources.

Government funding is in flux and while other avenues of funding are available, competition for foundation and corporate funds has never been more intense. In short, finding the funds will take optimum strategy, research, creativity, and, most of all, tenacity.

References

"Annotated List of State Foundation Directories." *Funding Review*, January-March 1981, *1* (2), 38–41, 52–54, 60.

Barkan, F., and Slade, R. "Data for Dollars." *The Grantsmanship Center NEWS*, March/April 1981, *9* (2), 29–37.

"The Bucks Stop Here." *The Grantsmanship Center NEWS*, March/April 1981, *9* (2), 4–5, 92–94.

Corporate Foundation Profiles. New York: The Foundation Center, 1980.

Corporate Fund Raising Directory. New York: Public Service Materials Center, 1980.

Dermer, J. (Ed.). *Where America's Large Foundations Make Their Grants*. New York: Public Service Materials Center, 1980.

"Developing Successful Proposals in Women's Educational Equity." *Trainers Manual, WEEAP (Women's Educational Equity Act Project)*. Washington, D.C.: U.S. Department of Education, 1979.

Dun and Bradstreet. *Million Dollar Directory*. Parsippany, N.J.: Dun's Marketing Services, 1980.

Dun and Bradstreet. *Reference Book of Corporate Managements*. New York: Dun and Bradstreet, 1981.

Federal Grants and Contracts Weekly. Washington, D.C.: Capitol Publications, Inc., May 19, 1981.

"FIPSE: Bureaucratic Bird That Flies Right." *Funding Review*. Jan/Mar. 1981, *1* (2), 16–19.

Foundation Center Publications and Services Catalog. New York: The Foundation Center, Spring, 1981.

Foundation Center Source Book Profiles. New York: The Foundation Center, 1979, 1980, 1981.

Foundation Directory. (Seventh Edition.) New York: The Foundation Center, 1979.

Foundation Grants Index, 1980. New York: The Foundation Center, 1981.

Foundation Grants to Individuals. (Second Edition.) New York: The Foundation Center, 1979.

Foundation News: The Journal of Philanthropy. Washington, D.C.: Council on Foundations, bimonthly.

Hillman, H. *The Art of Winning Corporate Grants*. New York: Vanguard Press, 1980.

Kurzig, C. M. *Foundation Fundamentals: A Guide for Grantseekers*. New York: The Foundation Center, 1980.

"Laying the Groundwork for Foundation Funding." *Government Product News,* May 1981, pp. 20-22.

Lefferts, R. *Getting a Grant: How To Write Successful Grant Proposals.* Englewood Cliffs, N.J.: Prentice-Hall, 1978.

Standard and Poor. *Register of Corporations, Directors and Executives.* New York: Standard and Poor, 1981.

U.S. Department of Commerce. *Commerce Business Daily.* Washington, D.C.: U.S. Government Printing Office daily publication.

U.S. General Services Administration. *Federal Register.* Washington, D.C.: U.S. Government Printing Office daily publication.

United States Government Manual. Washington, D.C.: U.S. Government Printing Office, annual.

U.S. Office of Management and Budget. *Catalog of Federal Domestic Assistance.* Washington, D.C.: U.S. Government Printing Office, 1980.

Twila C. Liggett is assistant director for acquisitions and development at the Great Plains National Instructional Television Library, a service agency of the University of Nebraska-Lincoln. Prior to her current position, she developed proposals and administered funded projects in the areas of reading and women's legal, social, employment, and educational equity.

Effective proposal writing involves developing a
persuasive message, understanding the key functions
of the proposal, and knowing the value of good
proposal organization. Armed with a creative idea, a
well-written proposal, and solid organizational and
community support, the proposal writer should be
able to maximize the opportunities for funding.

Writing the Proposal

Richard G. Maybee

A written proposal serves several functions in its overall role as a document for making funding decisions. First, it is most often the primary vehicle for persuasively communicating the project concept to the funding agency decision-makers. This involves an assertive approach to writing and organizing with strong emphasis on a positive portrayal of proposed action. That it should be persuasive suggests a clear, concise document with strong visual impact. Second, the proposal is in effect a plan of action and should be prepared with that definition in mind. As a plan of action, it should be specific as to measurable objectives, methods, time frames, and assignments of responsibilities. For most government proposals it is better to overstate rather than understate these points. Third, the proposal is a legal document which constitutes an offer by the applicant to perform the work of the project as stated. If accepted, even with modifications by the funding agency, it constitutes a binding agreement involving the scope of work, the dollar value paid by the funding agency and, where appropriate, the amount contributed by the applicant.

Decision Criteria

Before proposal development proceeds too far, it is necessary to specify the criteria against which the proposal will be evaluated in the decision-making process. For government grants, these criteria will be

J. Buskey (Ed.). *New Directions for Continuing Education: Attracting External Funds for Continuing Education,* no. 12. San Francisco: Jossey-Bass, December 1981.

stated in the final rules and regulations published in the *Federal Register* or other official publications. For private funding sources, they will be in letter form or available verbally from an official of the organization. Sometimes decision criteria will be quite general and it will be up to the prospective applicant to research prior giving patterns or talk to agency representatives. In any case, the needs addressed by the funding agency should be the same as those of the prospective applicant or this initial mismatch will severely reduce the likelihood of funding. The decision criteria are typically of two kinds: (1) procedural—dealing with what must be included in the application and what form it should take; and (2) programmatic—concerned with the quality of the program proposed and its conformity to the intent of the funding legislation or to the policy of the funding source. Some inferences can be made from the programmatic criteria that can help in writing the goals of the proposed project. Again, the greater the conformity between the goals of the project and the needs of the funding source, the greater likelihood there is that the applicant will receive funding.

Goals-Objectives-Activities (G-O-A)

It is suggested that the goals-objectives-activities (*G-O-A*) section of the proposal be written before any other major sections. The reason for this is that once the program goals are determined, all other features of the proposal can be organized around the goals. A goal, as viewed here, is a highly abstract, short, and unattainable but desirable condition. Its key is the use of an abstract value-oriented term. For example, a goal that would "increase the appreciation of the arts" in a given community would have as its abstract term the word *appreciation*. As a rule of thumb, three to four goals are typical for most projects. Some considerations are: (1) different target groups to be served by the project; (2) project staff qualifications and organization of work groups; and (3) realistically manageable project phases or components. More complex projects may need more goals to provide for more operational components.

Each goal is best supported by several *objectives*. An objective is defined as a time-bound, outcome-oriented, measurable condition. Following the example of the goal above, one objective might read: "by the end of the project year, 3,000 citizens will have attended one outdoor musical/stage event sponsored by the project." Another objective for the same goal might state: "within the first four months of the project 100 members of the community will become involved in planning some form of arts-related programs for the current year." Note that neither of these objectives states exactly *how* they are to be accomplished. This is left to the activities statements supporting each objective. Objectives begin to define the direc-

tion the applicant is taking in attempting to attain the goal. Objectives should be written to reflect a number of factors:
- Cultural and social environment,
- Physical, human, and material resources available,
- Community values,
- Organizational mission and role in the community,
- Other constraining factors such as budget limitations.

Thus far, the G-O-A might look like this:

Goal 1. To increase the appreciation of the arts in the community.
  Objective 1.1: By the end of the project year, 3,000 citizens will have attended one or more musical/stage events sponsored by the project.
  Objective 1.2: Within the first four months of the project, 100 members of the community will become involved in planning some form of arts-related programs for the current year.

The addition of activities under each objective will round out the G-O-A section. An activity is a statement which includes how the objective will be reached. It may take a number of activities to accomplish a single objective. For example, under Objective 1.1 above, Activity 1.1.1 might read "form committee to plan and organize four musical/stage productions during the project period." Activity 1.1.2 might read "contact community businesses for support of events totaling not less than $6,000." As objectives support goals, so activities support objectives. A hierarchical organization builds from the top down, letting the goals become the major organizers and the objectives the subordinate organizers. How it will be done is described by the activities. In the activities section is where the innovation and creativity of the applicant organization can shine forth. It is in the activity statements where the approach of one project is differentiated from that of other projects. Often, the more unique the pattern of activities, the greater likelihood of gaining the attention of the funding agency. The G-O-A section usually follows the needs section in the proposal.

The Group Process as an Aid to Writing the Proposal

Groups can contribute significantly to the quality of a proposal. Staff, policy, and advisory boards can provide different perspectives leading to the final project concept. Generally, policy boards or advisory groups will be responsible for establishing the organization's priorities and mission. Project goals can be developed from these priorities so long as they are consistent with the needs of the funding agency. It is important to discuss the concept of the specific project with policy, advisory, and staff groups, however, the actual writing of the goals is best done by one individual. Once written, the goals should be reviewed by the policy group, or its executive committee, to insure agreement with the organization's mission. Objectives are best written in consultation with a few project staff and organizational leadership for they are limited by resources, mission and direction desired.

The raw material for activities is best generated by a group brainstorming process. It is within this process that the limits of the individual can be transcended and the creative power of the group tapped. All too often, advisory or leadership groups are not asked for a structured input to the *how* of accomplishing organizational missions. The key is a structured input. Unstructured groups will agree with almost anything that is suggested; they are not challenged in ways that can help focus their thinking. A structured brainstorming approach can make the difference. How does it work? First, the objectives are written down. Second, each objective is defined by the group so that all agree on what is meant by the objective statement. Third, a two-minute time limit to generate activities for each objective is set and idea generation begins. No positive or negative feedback is allowed. Craziness and "piggybacking" of ideas is encouraged. By all means, quantity is encouraged over quality at this point. Research shows that the greater the quantity, the greater the likelihood of a higher quality outcome. No explanations are allowed. All ideas must be written so that everyone can see what is being produced. It is the associations produced by this visual and auditory input that assist in producing the variety and quantity of ideas. Also recommended is the taping of the session for further reference and more careful interpretation. The value is great to both the feeling of morale and productivity of staff and advisory groups when they are involved. In terms of ownership of an idea, it is usually given up to the group and not held by specific individuals. That makes idea generation easier for the shyer members of the group. It can enhance group spirit. Also, in terms of time, the group can be very productive. For example, if a project has four goals, and a minimum of four objectives for each goal, the total is sixteen objectives. If four to eight strategies are produced for each objective, the result is a total of 64 minimum and 128 maximum activities. This is a large number of ideas for one or a few individuals to produce. If in the group brainstorming process, four minutes were allotted to each objective for producing the raw material for the activities, the total is sixty-four minutes. A short time indeed to gather input from many individuals.

Another idea about using the group for writing the proposal is to use one individual as a stylistic editor so that if different sections are prepared by different individuals, the sections appear to be written by the same person. Also, care must be taken at the early stages of proposal development to involve representatives of cooperating or participating organizations in discussions where their roles play an important part in the project. Failure to do this can have serious negative consequences later in the proposal preparation process, and may even sabotage future interorganizational relations. As a source of community values, the group can be invaluable. Hearing the concerns and fears as well as the needs and directions of other agencies is important for the proposal preparation staff of the applicant agency. It is better to write proposals that have the greatest opportunity of acceptance and adoption once funded, than to attempt to force unwilling cooperators to participate. Very often, if funding is denied and supporting agencies are really behind the project, local funds will materialize to carry it out in some manner.

Plan of Action/Program Narrative

This section involves the written justification and rationale for each of the objectives along with some greater detail on each of the activities previously stated in the G-O-A section. Depending on the procedural criteria, the plan/narrative section usually follows the G-O-A section. A good way of beginning the plan/narrative is to discuss briefly the general approach of the project. For any program or project there is a basis upon which the direction was made, the objectives were set, and the operational parameters managed. This discussion can take several paragraphs or several pages, depending upon how extensive the basis of the project.

Next, the plan/narrative section should be broken down into program components. Each component should be titled as a shortened version of the goal. For example, if a goal were "to provide for effective communication education of Red Cross volunteers," the program component might be entitled *Communication Education*. Some ways to help define a program component include: (1) the most workable management unit given staff organization; and (2) service to identifiable target audiences. Each program component will include the objectives and activities which best relate to it. The G-O-A section, if written well, provides a clear outline for the organization of each program component.

Thus, following the outline of the G-O-A section, each objective can be discussed and each activity under it discussed also. For the objectives, basic questions such as why it is realistic, when it should be completed in relation to other objectives, and what are the restrictions on its implementation, should be answered. The discussion need not be long. When extra space is needed, it should be taken to fully justify the reasonableness of the objective.

For each activity, the narrative should describe what is going to happen, when it is going to happen, and who is responsible for making it happen and carrying it out. The most important question to be answered for each activity is what resources will be needed, both from the grant and from the participating organizations. There need not be detailed enumeration of these resources for each activity but sufficient examples should be given to provide the reviewer with an adequate understanding of the scope of resources needed. Failure to provide the scope of resources at this point can lead the reader to confusion over resources listed in the budget section of the proposal. Discrepancies must not occur between the resources needed for carrying out the project activities and those related in the budget. This is a common failure of many proposals. Where applicable, potential restrictions in carrying out the objectives should be mentioned and how they will be dealt with. Use "if such and such a problem should occur" rather than "when it occurs." Depending on the guidelines, the evaluation section and/or the time-line may be placed next within the plan/narrative. Each will be discussed separately as part of the management plan.

Management Plan

There are several options for the location of the management plan. In some proposals, all or parts of it can be located within the plan/narrative. In others, it may stand alone. In yet other forms of proposals, each part may be considered separately as a minisection in the body of the proposal. Regardless, there are some typical subsections of the management plan that bear discussing.

Time Line. Time lines are usually required in some form in most proposals. They provide the reader with the chronology of events, most easily organized by the groups of activities under each objective. Some variations include the name or title of the person most responsible for carrying out the activity. Figure 1 is one variation of a time line.

Evaluation Plan. As with time lines, evaluation plans are usually required in some form. They can range from the simple to the complex and highly technical. Much will depend upon the guidelines of the funding agency and the nature of the project. There are several elements which should be considered when writing evaluation plans. First, there should be

Figure 1. Time Line

Activity	Project Month											
	1	2	3	4	5	6	7	8	9	10	11	12
Objective 1.1 Attendance at Arts Events 1.1.1 Form Planning Committee (Project Director)	XX											

a discussion in narrative or outline form of the way in which formative evaluation will take place. Formative evaluation involves the ongoing assessment of progress toward the objectives and can include checklists, weekly staff meetings, and other in-progress measures of accomplishment. These assessments are used to make adjustments in order to maintain time-line events. Summative evaluation involves a collection of information over the project time period and uses that information to make an historical account of project achievements and failures. It is usually written in the last month of the project. Evaluation can be carried out by project staff, community members, advisory boards, clients, students, participants, and others involved with the project. External consultants can also be used to provide a more objective and where appropriate, technical evaluation. Their use should be carefully justified in the narrative and detailed in the budget. One way to portray the evaluation plan in the proposal is to include a discrepancy analysis chart. Such a chart can be used for both summative and formative evaluations. The discrepancy analysis format allows for stating overaccomplishments as well as underaccomplishments and the action which was taken to respond to the discrepancy. An example of a completed discrepancy analysis chart is shown in Figure 2. In a proposal, only columns one and two would be filled out.

Internal Organization Relationships. In this section, several items should be discussed. First is the schematic diagram of the project staff/agency hierarchy—the organization chart for the project. A standard line and block chart like that in Figure 3 is quite acceptable. Second, position responsibilities should be listed for each staff type. It is good to describe each of these responsibilities with a verb, for example, "supervises all project staff" would describe a responsibility of the project director. Third, any other organization departments or sections that will internally relate to the project should also be discussed.

External Organization Relationships. It is here that cooperating and participating agencies are discussed as to their role and degree of involvement with the project. It is a good idea to provide a diagram of the nature of these relationships showing advisory groups as well as the larger

Figure 2. Discrepancy Analysis Chart

Objective/ Activity	Accomplishment	Discrepancy	Analysis +/-	Action Taken
1.1 3,000 attend one concert or stage event	3,800 attended	800	+	Used additional income to offset event expenses.

Figure 3. Organization Chart

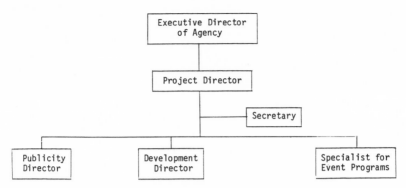

organizational structure. This section provides the "big picture" for readers so they have a full context in which to see the operation of the project.

Dissemination Plan. Not always required, but useful, the dissemination plan provides the reader with a discussion on how the project will make itself known to the community and/or the professional field to which it is related. Such items as use of media, publications, newsletters, conferences, attendance at professional meetings, and articles for professional journals are all typical of dissemination plans. This section need not be extensive but simply descriptive of a planned approach to information dissemination.

Organizational Capability. This is no place for modesty. If the reader is ever going to know your capacity to carry out the project, this is the place to be positive about it. There are several subparts that can be used to construct this section of the proposal. First is the listing with brief narratives of the relevant organizational accomplishments which have led to the creation of the proposed project. This may take several pages, but it must be done well with short headings for each accomplishment. Much of this type of information should be part of any agency's annual report. At least it could be done in advance of the final stages of proposal writing. Second, brief resumes of the major project staff should be provided. These should not be longer than one page in length. Full vitae should be available in the appendix and mentioned where deemed appropriate. Be sure to list the title of the staff member along with the name so the reader will have a clear basis to judge qualifications. Third, letters of support and commitment can be included in this section if there are not too many. Each letter might address such questions as :

- How is the need perceived by the supporting agency?
- What specifically is the supporting agency willing to commit to the project in terms of resources—human, material, equipment?

- How does the supporting agency see the project benefiting their own organization and constituency, as well as the community?

Often, these letters can be obtained as the full proposal is being written. A concept paper or abstract which would describe the project in general might be used to send to participating agencies.

Required and Optional Sections, Appendices. Sometimes special sections will be required in a proposal. These might be answers to technical questions, supporting needs assessment documentation, or other similar items. Locate the special section after the program narrative or management plan. Special sections can also be created by the proposal writer to deal with specific issues or concerns within the context of the project. Appendices should be as brief as possible. In fact, it is highly desirable to do without them altogether. Each appendix should be separated with a face sheet or tab.

Need/Problem

This section is written after the goals and after the plan/narrative. The reasoning behind this is that once it is determined what should be done and why that is realistic, it is much easier to focus the writing on only those needs truly relevant to the proposed project. Writing them first often results in much more elaboration than necessary and frequently more needs are described than the project can possibly deal with. Noting more needs than can be met confuses the reader with the scope and purpose of the project. Consistency is the best approach. If there are three goals, then there should be three identifiable needs emerging from the needs discussion. The identifiable needs could well be subparts of one major, overall need, or they might be three clearly separate and distinct needs. In any case, it is important to identify for the reader the specific premises which the goals, and subsequently the program components, are designed to fulfill. The program components in the plan/narrative should match the goals and their antecedent needs. Diagramatically, this might appear as follows:

Need 1 ---------------------------- Goal 1-------------- Program Component 1
Need 2 ---------------------------- Goal 2-------------- Program Component 2
Need 3 ---------------------------- Goal 3-------------- Program Component 3
(written third)   (written first)   (written second)

One way of organizing the needs section is to touch on the national or state legislation creating the funding program first. Study reports prepared for congressional committees often contain data which support the intent of the legislation, and such data can be used in a proposal. Next, the regional aspects of the need and then the state level aspects of the need can be discussed. Key data of a dramatic nature are very useful within these discussions. Last, the local need should be discussed in some detail. Quotes from those affected by the project are appropriate as well as opinions from local authorities and experts. The best basis for arguments in the needs section will be those from sources of authority. Data alone will not convince readers. A good discussion of the area involved in the project including demographics, economics, social, and cultural features is desirable after the local need is stated.

Proposal Continuity

One of the problems of writing grant proposals is to keep different sections continuous with others. One approach has been developed by the author where continuity worksheets are used to assist the proposal writer in maintaining consistency within the proposal. The sample worksheets shown in Figure 4 are provided as a general guide to the writer.

When displayed horizontally on letter size paper, there usually is room to provide sufficient detail for the reader to follow along easily. In addition, use of a numbering system showing relationships between each column on each sheet greatly facilitates tracking a specific concept through from beginning to end. The worksheets are usually used as planning documents from which the proposal narrative is written, however, they can be used in the proposal in lieu of a lengthy narrative, depending on the funding agency's requirements.

Proposal Writing Tips

Writers have their own styles which should not be suppressed, unless they are negative or pessimistic. More important than anything, the proposal should have a very positive tone—one that suggests forward thinking, creativity, innovation, and action. The choice of tense and verbs can make the difference between a merely descriptive proposal and a persuasive one. Action-oriented verbs are best with little use of the passive voice. Listed below are a number of "tips" for the proposal writer.

1. Break up the narrative with paragraph headings which cue the reader to the contents. Readers can then decide whether they want to read that part or go on to the next.

2. Don't beat a point to death. State it, support it, elaborate where necessary, and move on to the next point. Conciseness is highly desirable.

3. Refer but don't repeat. Refer ahead or back but try not to repeat information in the proposal unless specifically requested.

4. Avoid equivocal language. Such words as might, should, ought, could, may, possibly, hope, or maybe, are better replaced with words such as can and will.

Figure 4. Continuity Worksheets

1. Needs Statement: Part A

1.1 Concise Statement of the Problem (Use a simple sentence or short paragraph)	1.2 Background of the Problem (Causes and significance)	1.3 Current Status of the Problem (Document the current situation)

1. Needs Statement: Part B

1.4 Implications of the Problem (What will happen if nothing is done?)	1.5 Overview of Proposed Solution (State how proposal will alleviate the problem)	1.6 Organization of Proposal (Brief description of how proposal is organized)

2. Goals/Objectives/Plan of Action

2.1 Goal(s)	2.2 Objectives	2.3 Methods/Activities

3. Evaluation Plan

Objective No...	3.1 Data to be Gathered (What is being measured?)	3.2 Measure to be Used (Instruments/ methods for collecting data)	3.3 Data Collection Activities (Where, when, who will collect?)

4. Dissemination Plan

4.1 Analysis of Results (From evaluation plan)	4.2 Dissemination Activity Format	4.3 Target Audience	4.4 Anticipated Response/ Outcome

52

Figure 4 (continued)

5. Management/Personnel Plan

Methods/Actvitives/ Procedures No. . .	Staff Assignment	Percent of Time	Training Needs	Budget

5. Use plenty of transitions. Always keep the readers in touch with where they have been, where they are now, and where they are going.

6. Good visuals can enhance a proposal. Usually, visuals in the form of diagrams, flow charts, graphs, and tables (when simply stated) will increase the dramatic appeal of a proposal. Be sure to provide a good analysis in the narrative when charts depicting data are provided, otherwise the reader may become confused, wonder what the figures mean, and why they were included. This is a quick way to lose credibility in the minds of readers.

7. Use outline formats wherever possible to make the proposal more readable.

8. Edit and proofread carefully. There is no excuse for a sloppy proposal. Misspellings, typos, bad grammar, and improper word usage are a clear indication to the reader of organizational incompetency. Editors are worth their hourly wage to keep you out of trouble on these points.

9. Share proposal drafts with others. Reactions from individuals who know little about the project are very valuable. They are closer to the true role of the proposal reviewers than anyone else. Heed their comments and concerns.

10. Be careful when using humor. Inappropriate use of humor can ruin a proposal rather quickly. Avoid it if at all possible. A proposal is a serious document and most readers treat it accordingly.

11. Use the jargon of the funding source correctly. The language of a given program is important. If you are not familiar with it, talk to those who are. Internalize it so it is naturally a part of your thinking. As you write you will then be more likely to use it appropriately.

12. Fill out all forms correctly. Often in the rush of finishing a proposal, forms are not completed correctly. Be sure you have followed the directions to the letter. If there are questions, call the funding agency. Be sure to include correct signatures on all forms that require them. Failure to do this could disqualify your proposal.

13. Mail and deliver on time. There is no excuse for not meeting the deadline. Most federal programs disqualify you if you do miss it. Check out all mailing requirements well in advance. Check local closing times and procedures. If you use a private courier service realize that the only guaran-

tee is the price of delivery. They will not pay the lost funds you requested when you missed the deadline.

14. Bind securely. Do not use expensive bindings, expecially the three-ring type. All that is needed is a simple glue type or plastic prong type. Try not to make the binding increase the original size of the proposal.

15. Color code the proposal sections. They can make the proposal have higher visual impact as well as alert the reader to the beginning and ending sections without using tabs. Use colors that are appealing, not shocking. Employ color coding only when you have control of producing all copies needed by the funding agency.

Other Proposal Preparation Systems

There are alternative ways to write proposals, and several other authors have written books or pamphlets on one or more aspects of proposal preparation, including some for specialized audiences or types of projects. Among the more useful publications are those by Hall (1977), Kiritz (1979), and Krathwohl (1977). Krathwohl's book is specifically directed to writers of behavioral science research proposals, while the publications by Hall and Kiritz are useful primarily to those who write program and community service proposals.

Summary

Experience is the best teacher when writing proposals. It is a good idea to seek assistance from someone who has had experience in writing proposals that were funded. It is best to write with honest convictions and not try to oversell your concept. Readers appreciate honesty and conciseness along with quality ideas.

References

Hall, M. *Developing Skills in Proposal Writing*. (Second Edition.) Portland, Ore.: Continuing Education Publications, 1977.
Kiritz, N. J. "Program Planning and Proposal Writing, Expanded Version." *The Grantsmanship Center News*, May/June 1979, 5 (3), 33–79.
Krathwohl, D. R. *How to Prepare a Research Proposal*. (Second Edition.) Syracuse, N.Y.: Syracuse University Bookstore, 1977.

Richard G. Maybee is director of government, corporate and foundation relations at Guilford College in Greensboro, North Carolina. He has conducted numerous workshops and seminars on proposal writing and grant development and is a trainer for the National Grant Development Institute of Pocatello, Idaho.

Budgeting is more than a mystery,
less than a science.
In this nether world, budgeting
skill must be practiced
until it becomes art.

Project Budgeting:
A Six-Step Approach

Lynn H. Willett

The task of project budgeting requires a balancing act between the needs of the continuing education project to maximize its resources and the resource limitations of the funding agency. This balancing act requires art, skill, and knowledge of management science on the part of the project developer. Most budgets for permanent or temporary organizations require a variety of revenue sources to achieve the appropriate level of funds to carry out a complex project. One source of revenue which must be carefully described and defined is the money which is being requested from the funding agency. This detailed listing is called the *expenditure budget*. A six-step approach to project budgeting is offered to assist the project planner in building a budget which meets the needs of both the applicant and the funding agency. The budget process outlined relates specifically to one-year grant project requests as opposed to contracts. The steps in the proposed process are establishing project objectives, setting budget parameters, developing project time allocation estimates, identifying line-item expenditures, costing out non-personnel expenditures, and identifying matching sources of revenues.

J. Buskey (Ed.). *New Directions for Continuing Education: Attracting External Funds for Continuing Education,* no. 12. San Francisco: Jossey-Bass, December 1981.

Step One

The first step in a budget making process is to identify accurately and in detail the proposed project activities expressed in objectives and procedures. Only after the project has been conceptualized and written out can a realistic budgeting process be established. This phase of project planning will also help the continuing education administrator identify other available sources of revenue for the project. Typical sources are other institutional grants and contracts, contributions, project income or fees, and donations of services and supplies. Multiple-year funding requests will utilize this six-step process for only the first year. Subsequent years' budgets will be based on either incremental or zero-based budgeting, or some combination of the two approaches. Once the one-year project has been outlined and other resources identified, the administrator is now ready to establish budget expenditure parameters.

Step Two

The project director must make two budget expenditure parameter decisions. First, a decision must be made about the total amount of money which can be requested for the project, and second, the major budget categories for the project must be specified.

The major financial needs for the continuing education project emerge in the program conceptualization phase of step one. For example, while the administrator may feel that the project will require approximately $100,000 from a funding agency, it may not be realistic to submit a budget of that size if the funding agency has typically funded projects for only $50,000 each. The project developer must ask the funding agency what the average grant award is. This average and the range (low to high) of award amounts can be easily ascertained by examining the list of previously funded projects from the particular agency to which the application will be submitted. By analyzing these data, the project developer will quickly decide the total amount which can be requested. Then, the next parameter decision can be made.

Most continuing education project budgets can be broken down into three general categories. The first category is personnel. This category will account for the largest amount budgeted, and most continuing education projects will expend 70 percent to 80 percent of the requested funds in the personnel category. Full- and part-time salaries, consultants, and fringe benefits comprise the expenditure items in this category. The second general category is nonpersonnel items. These expenditures are viewed as essentially supportive items such as supplies, equipment, and travel. The nonpersonnel amount total is usually 15 percent to 25 percent of the total budget. The personnel and nonpersonnel amounts added together result in what is known as the *total direct costs* of the project. The final budget parameter which must be established is *indirect costs*. Indirect costs are viewed as overhead costs of the organization. The method for calculating an organization's indirect cost rate is explained in the chapter on federal regulations. As a rule of thumb, the indirect cost rate for most continuing education projects is 8 percent of the total direct costs requested.

At the end of step two, the project director will have a general total project amount determined and will have subdivided the total amount into three general expenditure categories. The next step in the budgeting process will be to translate project activities into allocations of personnel time.

Step Three

An accurate program time allocation breakdown will help the project administrator determine how staff will spend their time, and will result in well-developed job descriptions. The best approach to translating the project description into a time allocation breakdown is to use the logic of the program-planning-budgeting-system (PPBS) which itemizes the personnel needed to complete each project objective. A worksheet with several columns should be laid out which establishes for each objective the following information: number of staff required to complete the objective, amount of time needed for each staff, and nonpersonnel expenditures. For example, an objective dealing with the development of curriculum for a seven instructional hour continuing education course in "Reducing Stress for Emergency Room Nurses" would have the following time commitment estimates: supervision (project director), twelve hours; faculty (curriculum developer), thirty-two hours; secretarial, six hours; consulting, four hours; editing, two hours; graphic artist, six hours. Examples of nonpersonnel expenditure notations might include: one ream of paper, 400 Xerox copies, graphic art supplies, 4 overhead transparencies, and 200 miles of travel by the consultant. During step three, the project developer must have a clear understanding of what the allowable costs are from the viewpoint of the funding agency. For the federal government, OMB Circulars No. A-21, A-87, and A-122 identify allowable costs for federal grants. (See the chapter on federal regulations for a detailed discussion.) For awards from other sources, the administrator should contact the specific state agency, private foundation, or federal contractor to determine allowable costs. Once this detailed time breakdown has been performed on each project objective, the next step is converting time to dollars.

Step Four

Most project budgets are broken down into line-item budgets. These line-items are specific expenditure categories in which similar expenses have been lumped together. For *personnel*, each regular full-time or part-time position becomes a single line-item, but staff benefits for such staff are put together into one line-item known as *fringe benefits*. Translating the time of staff into personnel line-item expenses requires a careful determination of how many staff the project can afford. Once the determination of the number of staff required is made, the next task is to set appropriate salaries. If the proposed project is for a new organization outside an existing permanent organization, the project developer will have to survey existing community agencies to find out comparable salaries for secretaries, project administrators, teachers, and other staff. If the project is a part of an established permanent organization, state and federal agencies require that salaries given to grant personnel must be consistent with salaries given to similar personnel in the permanent organization.

The next major line item is fringe benefits which usually include health, dental, and life insurance, social security, unemployment compensation, and retirement plans. Most organizations' business offices are able to give a project developer a salary percentage figure which can be used to cover fringe benefit costs.

The last component in personnel is *contract services*. This line-item includes fee paid for consultants, legal and auditing services, public relation services, and for printing work which may be performed. Many state and federal agencies establish limitations on amounts which can be paid to consultants. Also, contractual agreement limitations are highly restricted in many agencies. The project developer should clarify with the agency staff what contractual limitations exist.

Step Five

After the personnel line-items have been finished, the project director now is ready to calculate the nonpersonnel costs. By examining the expenditure notations made in step three, a big step forward has been made. Space costs occur in projects which have to rent space from the permanent organization or from the community. Many projects, however, use space costs as an amount to match funds provided by the funding source. The amount paid for space rent must be no more than the local going rate in the particular community. This must be calculated on a per-square-foot basis, multiplied by the rate, and put in the space line-item along with associated maintenance and utilities expenses as shown in Figure 1.

Equipment is a line-item which is often overlooked by project developers. Several kinds of equipment, such as desks, chairs, filing cabinets, and calculators are needed just to get the project started.

Most federal and state agencies do not look favorably on equipment purchases and instead recommend equipment rental. Rental rates must be comparable to the area's rates for similar equipment. Many organizations

Figure 1. Budget Example

ITEM	AMOUNT REQUESTED	AMOUNT MATCHING	TOTAL
A. PERSONNEL			
1. Staff			
a. 1 Project Director @ $1200/mo. x 100% of time x 12 mos.	$14,400		$14,400
b. 1 Asst. Project Director @ $1000/mo. x 100% time x 12 mos.	12,000		12,000
c. 1 Secretary @ $700/mo. x 100% time x 12 mos.	8,400		8,400
d. 1 Vice President @ $2000/mo. x 20% time x 12 mos.		$ 4,800	4,800
Sub-Total $34,800	$34,800	$ 4,800	$39,600
2. Fringe Benefits			
a. State Unemployment Insurance and Workman's Compensation (6.2% of salaries, $39,600)	$ 2,157	$ 298	$ 2,455
b. Other benefits and contributions (FICA, health and life insurance) 12.9% of salaries, $39,600.	4,489	619	5,108
Sub-Total . . . .$ 6,646	$ 6,646	$ 917	$ 7,563
3. Contractual Services			
a. 5 On-site evaluation days @ $100/day	$ 500		$ 500
b. Audit Service - 8 days @ $150/day	1,200		1,200
c. Consultant: 1 Curriculum Developer @ $1000/mo. x 50% time x 10 mos.	5,000		5,000
d. Consultants: 3 Instructors @ $1100/mo. x 40% time x 9 mos.	11,880		11,880
Sub-Total $18,580	$18,580		$18,580
Sub-Total (Personnel). $60,026	$60,026	$ 5,717	$65,743
B. NON-PERSONNEL			
1. Facility			
a. 1000 sq. ft. @ $5.20/sq. ft. for 12 mos.		$ 5,200	$ 5,200
b. Maintenance & Custodial @ $45/mo. x 12 mos.		540	540
2. Equipment			
a. 3 desk rental @ $25 each/mo. x 12 mos.		$ 900	$ 900
b. 2 typewriters rental @ $32 each/mo. x 12 mos.	$ 384	384	768
c. 3 three-drawer filing cabinets @ $15 each/mo. x 12 mos.	270	270	540
3. Consummable Supplies (paper, pencils, etc.)			
$100 x 4.5 FTE Staff	$ 450		$ 450
4. Travel			
a. Local Staff Travel @ .19¢/mile x 2400 miles annual	$ 456		$ 456

Figure 1 (continued)

ITEM	AMOUNT REQUESTED	AMOUNT MATCHING	TOTAL
B. NON-PERSONNEL (continued)			
b. Out-of-State - One 3-day trip to Washington, DC (airfare $285 coach, plus $60 per diem)	465		465
5. Other			
a. 1 telephone ($35 installation, service $25/mo. x 12 mos.)	$ 335		$ 335
b. Postage, books, fees, printing	350		350
Sub-Total (Non-Personnel)	$ 2,710	$ 7,294	$10,004
TOTAL DIRECT COSTS	$62,736	$13,011	$75,747
C. INDIRECT COSTS			
Calculated @ 8% of $75,747 (direct costs)	$ 5,018	$ 1,042	$ 6,060
TOTAL PROJECT BUDGET	$67,754	$14,053	$81,807

use equipment as a matching item. Consumable supplies which include paper, pencils, and teaching materials, are very difficult to estimate. As a rule of thumb, use $100 per full-time equivalent staff member per year. For projects which will be purchasing large amounts of special teaching materials, these should become a separate line-item in the budget category. Travel must be broken down into local and out-of-state line-items. The estimated number of miles per month traveled is multiplied by the local mileage reimbursement rate multiplied by the number of project months. Out-of-state travel must be shown separately and in some cases justified in appended budget narratives. For out-of-state travel, the number of trips, destinations, local per diem allotment and cost of transportation should be provided.

Telephone cost is often overlooked but is a justifiable project expense. Project developers should calculate the installation cost as well as the monthly service charge and estimated long-distance charges. The final nonpersonnel line-item is a general catchall category labelled *other*. Examples of costs which should be considered and included here are: postage, insurance, dues to associations, subscriptions, printing and duplicating, and other publication costs such as addressing and mailing.

The final budget category which must be translated into money is the indirect cost category. This is determined as a percentage of either the salaries and wages of the project, or the total direct costs of the project. Federal agencies commonly limit the rate to eight percent of total direct costs for educational training grants, however, the applicant organization may have an approved audited rate that is somewhat higher. The audited rate is used for contractual arrangements or in instances where the federal agency does not have a specified maximum rate for grants. The project director will select the appropriate indirect cost rate and calculate the amount to be included in the project budget. (See Matelski's chapter on federal regulations for information on how to establish an indirect cost rate.) The indirect cost amount is a new line-item expense which is added to the total direct costs and results in a final overall project total cost. By completing step five, the project developer is now ready to show local financial support for the project.

Step Six

Most funding agencies, particularly for grants, require the identification of resources which the local agency can provide. The project developer should carefully review the project application materials to determine if a certain matching amount or in-kind contribution is required. This can vary from 0 to 50 percent. Matching funds means that the local agency is going to help offset the costs of the proposed project by contributing funds or services which have a specific dollar value. These amounts are shown by line-item and in most cases these amounts are auditable. In identifying the matching amounts, the project developer should examine what services the applicant agency will be providing the project. Typically, the permanent organization is providing facilities, equipment, general administrative supervision, supplies, and clerical assistance. These are line-item expenses which the applicant can generally use as a matching contribution. Other resources which can be shown as contributions are volunteer time on advisory committees, faculty time in reviewing or pretesting materials, help from other agencies, use of the local library, and expenses related to business services such as bookkeepers and data processers.

An often overlooked source of matching funds is the indirect cost incurred by the applicant organization. Normally, the applicant can claim a contribution of indirect costs on the matching funds provided by using the same indirect cost rate being applied to the funds requested from the funding agency. Alternatively, if the applicant has an audited indirect cost rate that is higher than the rate being allowed for a particular project, it is usually appropriate to use the difference between the allowed rate and the audited rate as a matching contribution. Sometimes the difference is substantial and can mean the difference between sufficient and insufficient matching funds.

Once the matching line-items have been identified and conservative estimates of costs have been established, the formal process of project budgeting has been completed. The next activity is to organize all of these data into a coherent picture.

Conclusion

Figure 1 displays all the budget information for a typical grant project application. After completing step six, the administrator will be able to put all of the information into an easily understandable form. Many agencies also require that budget data be summarized in general categories onto forms which they provide. In addition to displaying the budget as shown in Figure 1, it is always useful to provide a short precise narrative which is attached to the budget. This budget narrative should describe for each major category such as personnel, nonpersonnel, and indirect costs, any unusual expenditures or unique ways of calculating rates, mileage, or other factors. For example, if the project is going to use a research team to evaluate the project, describe in the project narrative how the contractual rate was determined.

Summary

The project director, by following a six-step approach to budget building, will accomplish both the translation of a program idea into a monetary action plan, and the creation of a useful mechanism which will serve as a tool for monitoring and controlling the project once it is funded.

References and Further Readings

Chamber of Commerce of the United States. *Financial Management Handbook for Associations*. Washington, D.C.: Chamber of Commerce of the U.S., 1973.

Conners, T. (Ed.). *The Non-Profit Organization Handbook*. New York: McGraw-Hill, 1980.

The Grantsmanship Book. Los Angeles: Grantsmanship Center, 1980.

Gross, M. *Financial and Accounting Guide for Non-Profit Organizations*. New York: Ronald Press, 1979.

Hall, M. *Developing Skills in Proposal Writing*. (Second Edition.) Portland, Ore.: Continuing Education Publications, 1977.

Nelson, C., and Turk, F. *Financial Management for the Arts*. New York: Associated Council for the Arts, 1975.

Sweeny, A., and Wisner, J. *Budgeting Fundamentals for Non-Financial Executives*. New York: American Management Association, 1975.

Lynn H. Willett is vice president for development and community services at Elgin Community College in Elgin, Illinois, and for ten years has been involved in resource development as a grantsman, teacher and writer.

Give them something to crow about,
but do it their way.

What Government Agencies Look for in Proposals

Donald A. Deppe

Government makes grants and enters into contracts for the continuing education of adults in order to achieve important public purposes. In this regard, government subscribes to the view held by most citizens that education is an indispensable tool for improving the human condition and advancing the ends of a free and healthy society.

Continuing education administrators hold equally high notions of the significance of their work. Along with government, they see the importance of designing and implementing continuing education programs. These programs will ensure, expand, or otherwise improve employment and employability, economic development, equal rights, social services, public safety, environmental quality, government operations, energy resource development and utilization, inter-group relations, and a number of other conditions that affect the quality of life in America.

That the purposes of government and continuing education coalesce at this level of generality is heartening. That diversions of purpose intrude, however, at the level of designing and implementing specific programs for which government support is sought, comes as a disheartening surprise to most administrators seeking such assistance for the first time. Facing the creative administrator's grand design for a new program that sparkles with innovation, flexibility, and great expectations is usually

J. Buskey (Ed.). *New Directions for Continuing Education: Attracting External Funds for Continuing Education,* no. 12. San Francisco: Jossey-Bass, December 1981.

an application form and instructions that moments ago were snatched abruptly from the hands of a startled mail clerk who still wonders why the plain brown envelope created such passionate interest.

The enthusiasm is short lived. Now crestfallen, the formerly eager administrator has just survived a first exposure to what is perceived as the arid legalese of enabling legislation, the rigid circumscriptions of program regulations, the unrealistic deadlines, the array of lines, blocks, and boxes for which alien information must be provided, and the inflexible format for presenting the program narrative.

At this point, the search for federal or state support of the project often ends in a short-sighted and defeatist conclusion that the gulf between the worlds of the prosaic bureaucrat and the progressive administrator can never be bridged.

The Principle of Enlightened Self-Interest

On the other hand, a bit of insight into the principle of enlightened self-interest may stimulate some creativity and produce a successful application. This comes about when the administrator conducts a critical assessment of the goals of the organization and decides how well the proposed project and government support will serve and enhance those goals. If the project idea remains vital and viable, the successful seeker of government funds focuses upon the challenge of the "getting-what-I-want-by-giving-them-what-they-want" procedure. It involves the melding of two sets of self-interests: the government getting what it needs to meet congressional intent, administration priorities, and agency recognition; and the continuing education administrator getting what is needed to advance the organization, create or expand a program, serve clients, and gain professional recognition.

When you realize that these interests can indeed match, the process of dealing with the once imposing application process becomes a manageable and nonthreatening process of give-and-take that benefits all parties involved.

None of this is meant to suggest that applicants must abandon creative ideas or that government is not interested in innovation. Administrators live by their bright inventions and many government agencies survive by supporting new approaches. In spite of limitations imposed by authorizing legislation, detailed regulations, bureaucratic compartmentalization, and political vagaries, government agencies do look for projects to support that are likely to enhance their own image, gain the admiration of congressional appropriation committees, satisfy constituents, and contribute ultimately to their own survival and growth as government entities. Give them something to crow about, but do it their way! Provide what is asked for in the order and format prescribed. You will find that you can do so and sacrifice few, if any, of the essential elements of your unique approach.

But What Do They Really Ask For?

Upon deciding in a given situation that the apparent interests of the granting agency and administrator coincide, what should you expect to encounter in terms of typical application requirements? The best way to answer this question is to obtain copies of application packages from the agency or agencies most likely to support projects in your areas of interest. You should examine the material carefully and pay particular attention to the following items that are likely to be found in a grant application:

The Authorizing Legislation. Here, in the language of public law, the intention of the lawmakers is expressed in terms of the amount of money authorized, the purpose(s) for which it is to be expended, the kinds of activities to be supported, and, usually, the kinds of programs and activities ineligible for support. Frequently, you must read no further to decide if a likely source of support has been identified.

Regulations. Based upon the law itself and its *legislative history*, the record of congressional hearings and debates produced prior to enactment, the regulations generally elaborate on the scope and purpose of the law, provide definitions of critical terms, spell out selection criteria, identify eligible applicants, specify information to be provided in applications, and describe allowable and nonallowable costs. The regulations, unless in a "proposed" status, have the same force and effect as law. Thus, since rulemaking is another form of lawmaking, it is important for the continuing education administrator to take advantage of opportunities that present themselves to shape proposed regulations.

Instructions. The instructions may repeat some portions of the regulations, but they will also contain very specific directions for completing standard face sheets or other printed forms on an item-by-item basis. In addition, the instructions will supply information about submission procedures, whom to contact for additional information, evaluation criteria, review procedures, narrative format, and procedures for notifying applicants of an award or rejection. The level of detail is sometimes minute, including page limitations, whether to single-space or double-space the narrative section, how to package the material, and what to put on the mailing label. Just remember—do it their way! In some cases a blank left empty or a departure from stipulated format is sufficient ground for rejecting the application without further review.

Selection Criteria and Review Procedures. On occasion, these items or evaluation criteria may be listed and discussed separately from the section on general instructions. In either case, they constitute critical clues for deciding the most effective way to present a narrative description of the proposed project. The criteria are usually weighted with assigned points for each. If time permits, it is helpful to ask a respected colleague to play the role of reviewer and, using the criteria provided, have that person read the application and provide a score for each criterion. Then, revise the application in those areas that are given low scores. Some writers are capable of sufficient objectivity to do this exercise on their own, but one way or another, it usually proves beneficial.

The Typical Federal Review Process

Federal agencies engage in a variety of procedures to evaluate applications and make awards. In some cases the process is entirely internal. Program and budget staff of a particular branch of the Department of Education, for example, will review applications, recommend grantees to a division director, who reviews and forwards recommendations to a deputy assistant secretary. This person then approves grants to be made in the name of the secretary.

In the same department, however, each eligible application to a different program may be reviewed, rated, and ranked by review panels which will include both federal and nonfederal experts. In this case, as in the former, judgments will be based on the criteria stated in the application package. Panel recommendations are forwarded eventually to a deputy secretary who, again, approves and announces awards in the name of the secretary.

The foregoing examples serve to indicate that the review process is one of two general types: *internal*, where decisions are made totally by staff, and *external*, where some staff involvement is present but the emphasis is placed upon a peer review. The most frequently adopted approach is the latter, and in some organizations like the National Endowment for the Humanities, procedures have been developed that ensure rigorous review by both staff and outside experts.

The endowment entertains approximately 11,000 proposals per year. Many are submitted first in draft form and reviewed by staff. The drafts are returned to the authors for revision in accordance with the suggestions made by staff. Upon return of the revised proposal to the endowment, the proposal is mailed to appropriate experts in the field (usually three and no more than six). These reviewers are chosen on the basis of the subject matter and proposed methodology. They provide written comments that are shared subsequently with members of a peer review panel.

The peer review panels are selected randomly by a computer from an automated list of 18,000 qualified panelists so as to minimize, if not eliminate, the "old-boy" syndrome of review by one's friends. The panels meet in Washington to review proposals and the comments of the outside experts. The panels then rate the submissions giving each one a total score based on specific criteria. Staff members of the endowment chair the panel meetings and enter into the deliberations actively.

Endowment staff members subsequently prepare abstracts of the proposals receiving the highest scores, and after taking budgetary constraints into account, submit these for consideration by the National Council on the Humanities at its next quarterly meeting. Subcommittees of the National Council meet one or two days before the plenary sessions to review the work of staff, outside experts, and the peer panels. The subcommittees prepare motions for the Council, and at the council meeting all members deliberate over the proposal summaries and recommended actions. Subcommittee members are called upon to provide additional information as needed. The full Council then takes formal action regarding the recommended disposition of each proposal, for example, approval, rejection, or deferral. Upon adjournment of the Council, the chairman of the endowment exercises final judgment and informs applicants of the outcome—invariably the outcome recommended by the Council.

The details of peer and staff review processes do differ in varying degrees among federal agencies, and among programs within an agency. The procedures are usually described in writing, and where this is not done, program staff will provide information about the process if asked. The important consideration is that few awards are made on political grounds. Virtually all submissions are reviewed rigorously, and the proposal writer should prepare material in light of the certain knowledge that it will be scrutinized carefully by persons at least equally knowledgeable in the matters under review.

State and Local Government Procedures

Continuing education administrators who look only toward Washington for government support overlook tremendous resources in their own backyard. Not only do local governments spend sizable local revenues, but they also make decisions on allocating billions of dollars in direct federal assistance. Twenty years ago this assistance amounted to $7 billion; in 1981 it will total $88 billion (Federal System, p. 1). By tapping this resource, one administrator received $85,000 in two years from city and borough governments alone to support art projects in her city (Derfner, 1975, p. 16).

State and local governments look for continuing education projects to support for reasons not too dissimilar from those enumerated for the federal government at the beginning of this chapter. The essential differences in dealing with government at the local rather than the federal level grow out of proximity and familiarity. Both are very real advantages.

The continuing education administrator is in a position to interact frequently with state legislators, department heads, members of state boards and commissions, county council members, city managers, and other key persons involved in the decision-making process. Many such persons are social as well as professional acquaintances. The working apparatus of local government is as familiar to the administrator as are the people who orchestrate policy and practice.

This closeness and familiarity with the people and workings of government make the application and review process more direct and intimate than is characteristic of one's dealings with the federal establishment. While many of the formal application procedures of state and local government parallel those of the federal agencies, the administrator of continuing education will find the following tasks easier and more productive at the local level:

1. Keeping abreast of which elected or appointed officials and community leaders are making or influencing key decisions in the grant and contract arena.
2. Capitalizing on the contacts of other people within one's organization such as the chief executive officer or members of the governing board or advisory committee.
3. Making one's program visible and becoming known as a leader in the field.
4. Finding opportunities to influence the establishment of spending priorities within programs that support or should support the education of adults.
5. Getting to know the persons directly involved in the application review process.

A particular element of the review process frequently used at state and local levels, but rarely a part of the federal procedure, is the requirement to appear before a decision-making body to provide oral defense and explanation of a proposal. It is important to prepare carefully for this presentation. Preparation includes not only being armed with supporting background data to answer possible questions, but being dressed appropriately to make a proper personal and professional impression.

The foregoing discussion does not mean that dealing with state and local government agencies involves "crass politics." Where dealings are direct and personal, and the key actors are well known in the community as well as to one another, the "practical politics" of human interaction are noticeably present and intense.

Working with people at the state and local level also helps in facilitating many applications for federal funds. For example, many proposals must undergo prior review and comment by groups of local citizens and officials before a federal agency will consider them. The review process implemented by OMB Circular No. A-95 is designed to allow state, regional, and local governments to integrate federal assistance with existing programs, policies and plans. See the chapter on federal regulations and Saasta (1975) for further information.

Capitalizing on Failure

Three crisis points are experienced after one catches the fever of seeking government support for continuing education activities. The first occurs upon reading the application package. The threat of death by disbelief wanes only when the patient agrees to do it their way. The second occurs during the struggle to meet an absolutely fixed deadline. Death by heart failure is averted only through the application of sheer stamina and the consumption of much midnight oil. The third, a notice of rejection, is most threatening of death by suicide. But please don't take the hemlock. There is much to learn through failure.

Upon being notified of rejection an unsuccessful applicant may take the following steps:

1. *Find out why the proposal was rejected.* Some agencies provide this information in writing as part of their customary practices. Others will provide it upon request.

2. *Revise the proposal and resubmit it.* Remove the reported weaknesses and further fortify even those points rated highly. Make the narrative more readable and compelling.

3. *Request reconsideration of the application.* Many agencies have formal procedures for filing an appeal of a rejection, but the decision to follow this procedure should be considered carefully, and used only when the applicant has unassailable evidence of unfair or unjust treatment. Human frailties considered, one runs the risk of damaging relationships with the funding agency and professional colleagues. Agency officials take umbrage at being challenged; colleagues more successful than yourself do not take budget cuts for their projects very kindly. The latter circumstance arises because projects are approved up to the limit of available funds. When someone appeals a negative decision successfully, the money required for that project must be taken from the budgets of those approved at an earlier date.

4. *Save the application.* In all likelihood the basic ideas in the proposal can be used to advantage in the future. In any event, you have developed a lot of basic material that will be useful again.

5. *Actively seek support elsewhere.* Upon reviewing agency reasons for rejection, you may discover that only budget limitations or unusually high competition led to rejection. Find an agency in which your project is given highest priority.

6. *File another application soon.* The rider thrown from a horse is advised traditionally to remount immediately. Don't allow the first failure

to paralyze you. A larger number of proposals are never funded because they are never written, in comparison to the number that are written and rejected. Keep on writing!

Projecting the Future

As this chapter is written, there is speculation and concern about the withering of federal programs that provide support for the kinds of activities in which continuing educators have an obvious interest. While details regarding these developments are not yet available, two general objectives of the current administration are very clear: to reduce federal spending and to return to the states the responsibility for the conduct and cost of matters increasingly viewed as no longer usefully subject to federal interference. In keeping with the former objective, state and local taxation may well rise, making this arena an increasingly promising source of external support for continuing education. As a result of the latter initiative, programs of categorical aid, for example, funds given to the states, but earmarked for very specific purposes, will dwindle, while growing emphasis will be placed on block grant programs in which states and localities have wide latitude in how the funds are spent. This development also points to increasing reliance of the continuing education administrator upon states and localities for support of needed projects.

In any event, government at all levels has a vested interest in the education of its citizens—youth and adults. It is unlikely that the competent administrator will face the total absence of public funds to achieve public goals. Do it their way, do it on time, and keep on doing it.

References

Derfner, C. "City Hall: An Important Resource for Your Organization." *The Grantsmanship Center News*, September/November 1975, *2* (5), 15–21.

Saasta, T. "A-95 Proposal Review Process." *The Grantsmanship Center News*, September/November 1975, *2* (5), 37–54.

"The Federal System in the 1980s: Money, Power and Responsibility." Congressional Research Service, Library of Congress, Issue Brief No. 81044, updated May 7, 1981.

*As program specialist for the U.S. Commission
on Civil Rights, Donald A. Deppe evaluates
proposals and the outcomes of resulting projects for
the commission's ten regional offices. He has held a
variety of posts in higher education and the
federal government, and has gained wide experience in
both obtaining and providing millions of dollars of external
support for continuing education activities.*

"There are few things more mysterious. . . .
The foundation process can be as random
and illogical as anything else in life." (Hartman and
others, 1974, p. 1).

What Foundations Look
For in Proposals

John H. Buskey

From the perspective of the grantseeker, the world of foundations is indeed mysterious, and part of the mystery lies in the fact that foundations are independent from one another and not subject to a common set of operational rules and regulations as are federal agencies. In addition, there are enormous variations among foundations as to size, location, interests, staff support, philosophy, and decision making processes. All of these factors contribute to the difficulty in finding a specific foundation that is most likely to provide support for a particular project, and in approaching that foundation effectively.

Data on assets and staff support serve to illustrate the diversity of foundations. In the United States there are approximately 28,000 independent foundations, of which 22,000 actively award grants. Foundation assets exceed $35 billion, and they currently award over $2.3 billion in grants annually. Only one hundred foundations have assets in excess of $50,000,000; they represent only one-half of one percent of the active foun-

The following contributed ideas and constructive criticism to a draft of this chapter: Edward Hirsch and Robert Sandberg of the University of Nebraska Foundation, Randall Bretz of the University of Nebraska-Lincoln, Richard Maybee, and Twila Liggett, who assisted in developing the basic outline for the chapter.

J. Buskey (Ed.). *New Directions for Continuing Education: Attracting External Funds for Continuing Education,* no. 12. San Francisco: Jossey-Bass, December 1981.

71

dations, yet control 48 percent of all foundation assets. At the other extreme, 19,000 foundations (86 percent) give away only seven percent of the funds awarded annually by foundations (Kurzig, 1980, pp. 17–18).

Relatively few foundations have full-time paid professional staff, and most rely on voluntary board members, family members, or trust officers of financial institutions for evaluating proposals, making awards, and monitoring the progress of projects. A recent Foundation Center survey, for example, found that only 626 of the 3,400 largest foundations had some type of staffing (Kurzig, 1980, p. 19).

Given the diversity of foundations, the variety of experiences that grantseekers report in their relations with foundations, and the growing literature in the field of external funding, the major purposes of this chapter are to introduce first the major issues related to seeking funds from foundations, and, second, the literature which will provide specific information. The issues to be discussed include researching foundations, approaching foundations, the characteristics of foundation proposals, and how foundations evaluate proposals and make awards.

Researching the Foundation

The first task in searching for foundation funds of any kind is to define the project by developing a concise written statement of the project idea. With a written idea in hand, you can then undertake the systematic search for potential funding sources described in Liggett's chapter.

Once you have a tentative list of foundation sources, narrow the list to those whose interests really match the project you have in mind. Kurzig (1980) suggests that the review of individual foundations should include collecting information on the obvious factors such as address, names of staff, officers and trustees, assets, purposes, range and average size of gifts, and application procedures. The list of grants awarded should then be reviewed with several questions in mind: Does the foundation have a commitment to funding in your subject field? Does it make grants in your geographical area? Does the foundation make grants in the range of the project you are proposing? Do they expect you to share the costs of the project? What types of organizations do they support? Are there specific deadlines for proposal submission? Much of this information can be gleaned from the documents listed in Liggett's chapter (this volume). Foundation annual reports, newspaper articles, and various journals on grantsmanship or fund raising are also important sources of current information. One should ask to be placed on foundations' mailing lists and try to develop linkages to foundation trustees or staff.

In considering which foundations to approach, it is well to consider first those in the community, then state, regional, and, finally, national foundations. The farther afield you go for funds, the less knowledgeable foundations are likely to be about your organization, and the less likely they are to have interests in your community.

In addition to Kurzig, Conrad (1976, 1977), Hillman (1980), and Malo (1977) have writen helpful materials on how to conduct research on foundations and other private sector sources.

How To Approach Foundations

Because of the diversity and independence of foundations, it is not possible to provide categorical rules about how to approach specific foundations and how to find out what individual foundations really look for in the proposals they receive. The experience of individual grantseekers varies widely and an effective approach to one foundation may not be effective with others.

The first two steps, as noted earlier, are to define the project accurately, clearly, and concisely, and to identify the specific foundations that are likely to support the kind of project proposed. The third step is to secure application forms or guidelines, and discover the specific application procedures. This step probably will involve personal or written contact with the foundation. The importance of cultivating personal contacts with foundation staff, trustees, and others knowledgeable about the foundation is sometimes underestimated by the novice grantseeker (Glass, 1980).

The fourth step is to submit a written document in the format desired by the foundation. Kurzig (1980) suggests that the larger foundations with staff usually prefer to receive a preliminary letter describing the proposed project so they can indicate early whether or not the topic is of interest to their foundation. According to Warm (1979), who has written a very informative article on approaching foundations, "the letter should include a brief description of your organization, verification of its tax-exempt status, a summary of the program for which funding is sought and a proposed budget" (p. 37). The letter should also request a meeting to discuss the project if desired. Conversely, the smaller foundations without staff would probably prefer to receive a full proposal, which may be in letter form (two to four pages long), thus eliminating the need to respond to numerous preliminary ideas (Kurzig, 1980).

Follow-up is important. If responses to your inquiries or proposals are not forthcoming in a reasonable time, it is appropriate to call, determine the status of the submission, and propose a meeting. Many foundations do not have the staff to see everyone, however, so they may prefer to communicate by phone or by mail.

If one is fortunate enough to be invited to a meeting to discuss the project idea or proposal, this means that the foundation is more than mildly curious about the project and that they are interested in discussing the project in detail. Warm (1979), Hillman (1980), and Conrad (1977), each describe in practical terms how to arrange meetings and the conduct in these meetings that will make most effective use of the limited time available.

Characteristics of a Foundation Proposal

In one sense, most proposals are alike and contain the same major elements. There are, however, significant differences between proposals for foundations in contrast to those for government agencies. One of the major differences lies in the public versus private nature of the two types of sources. Government agencies, because of the variety of "laws, rules, regulations, guidelines, forms, programmatic reports, and programmatic philosophies" (Lefferts, 1978, p. 117) which are subject to public scrutiny, provide an opportunity for the careful proposal writer to prepare applications that are responsive to specific agency interests and requirements.

As private agencies, foundations each have a set of guidelines and policies that are unique to the organization, and were either established by the donor(s) or by the board of directors. Foundations can, therefore, set their own parameters for programs to be supported, the geographical area they serve, the amounts to be awarded to applicants, and the types of organizations to which they will make awards. These criteria are not necessarily fully disclosed to prospective applicants.

Because most foundations do not provide detailed and specific guidelines on how to prepare proposals, proposal writers are often in the position of choosing a format and outline that best presents their project and their needs. If, however, a foundation does provide application information, one should be sure to follow the guidelines as closely as possible.

Experienced proposal writers tend, over time, to select a format and sequence that usually meets their needs, feeling free to modify it as the occasion requires. A good example of an effective system is the one presented by Maybee in the first chapter of this sourcebook.

An alternative format and sequence, consisting of eleven basic elements which should generally be addressed in any proposal to a foundation, is presented in Kurzig's book:

1. *Cover letter* on the organization's letterhead signed by its chief executive officer.
2. *Table of Contents.*
3. *Summary of the proposal,* no longer than one page and including the amount of money requested, the total project budget, the specific purpose of the grant, and the anticipated end result.
4. *Qualifications* of the organization and staff to carry out the program.
5. *Statement of the problem* or need addressed by the project.
6. *Goals and objectives of the program.*

7. *Methods* to be used to achieve the objectives, including a timetable for implementing the specific steps.
8. *Evaluation criteria* by which the program's effect will be measured.
9. *Budget.*
10. *Future funding* sources and plans.
11. *Appendix,* including evidence of tax-exempt status, supporting documents, references, etc. (Kurzig, 1980, p. 89).

To these elements, a title page should be added before the table of contents. Other writers have suggested different sequences of topics depending upon how they want to present specific issues, and of course, upon what they perceive the funding source's requirements to be. All of the issues listed above usually need to be addressed, and the proposal writer should order them appropriately for a particular presentation.

How Foundations Evaluate Proposals

Foundations annually receive nearly one million requests for funding, and probably no more than six or seven percent of the requests are actually funded (Kurzig, 1980, p. xiii). Thus, over ninety percent of proposals are rejected and foundations, of necessity, have become experts at saying "no."

The processes and criteria that foundations use to evaluate the numerous proposals they receive are unique to each foundation. In contrast to government agencies, the processes, procedures, and criteria employed by foundations are not public information and thus it is difficult to say with certainty how a given foundation may make decisions. Several authors, however, have written about the grantmaking processes of foundations in general, or the processes of a specific foundation.

A flow chart describing the grant administrative process as used by the Hill Family Foundation of Minnesota was published in an article by Bonine (1971, p. 247). The flow chart has eight major steps following the receipt of an application: (1) initial screening, (2) review by staff of foundation, (3) preparation of proposal for board action, (4) board action, (5) notification of applicant, (6) staff follow-up, (7) reporting by foundation and grantee, and (8) closing the file.

The evaluation process begins as soon as an inquiry is received and focuses on criteria relating to the applicant's eligibility, the amount of information provided, the relationship of the request to the foundation's policy and program interests, and the amount of the request in comparison to the foundation's normal grant awards. A large percentage of rejections occur in the first step because of obvious mismatches between the proposed project and the foundation's interests. Rejections also occur in both the second step, where detailed study of the application is made, and in the fourth step, when the foundation's board reviews proposals.

Other authors have written about the evaluation process. Lefferts, for example, suggests nine criteria to use in evaluating proposals: clarity, completeness, responsiveness, internal consistency, external consistency, understanding of the problem and service methods, organizational and staff capability, efficiency and accountability, and realism (1978). The anonymous corporate author of "I Hate Charities" presents "The Heartless 37-Point Checklist," which has three major components: the soliciting organization's character, the organization in relation to company policy, and the size of the gift (Anonymous, 1976). Hillman (1980), also writing about corporate grants, lists numerous questions under the following headings: "Is there a need for the project? Is the project relevant to us? Is the applicant qualified? Are the methods practical? Are the results measurable? What are the long-term implications?" He concludes with a list of "less-than-responsible criteria." Mayor (1972), an officer of the New York Community Trust, addresses the value systems used by foundations to evaluate proposals and suggests that the larger foundations will tend to consider the national impact of projects, while the smaller foundations may tend to look more at the value of the project on its own merits. Since foundations may expect or desire some continuing relationship with their grantees, it is usually appropriate in proposals to stress any existing or potential linkages between the proposed project and the goals and program of the foundation.

Several case studies of the grant making processes of foundations have been published. Among them are "How a Foundation Makes a Grant," a case study of a specific grant awarded by an anonymous, but real, foundation (Hartman, Mundel, and Shakely, 1974); "How Foundations Review Proposals and Make Grants," an interview with the executive director of the Chicago Community Trust (Saasta, 1976); "How the Ford Foundation Determines What (and Whom) It Will Support," an interview with the assistant secretary of the Foundation (Saasta, 1977b); "A Family of Family Foundations," an interview with the executive director of Joint Foundation Support (Saasta, 1977a); and a descriptive analysis of the "Beirne Foundation: The Untold Story of the Labor Movement" (Hallahan, 1979). These cases provide an enlightening insight into the internal processes of the foundations and show the range and scope of their interests and concerns.

Summary

The diversity and independence of foundations contribute to the folklore that has grown up around the foundation world. The proposal rejection rate is high and, therefore, it is incumbent upon grantseekers to do their research well, cultivate foundation prospects, and make effective presentations of well-executed proposals. Even the well-written proposal, however, will not succeed unless the proposed subject is of interest and significance to the foundation.

References

Anonymous. "I Hate Charities." *Grantsmanship Center News*, March/April 1976, *2* (7), 6–11.

Bonine, R. W. "One Part Science, One Part Art." *Foundation News*, November/December 1971, *12* (6), 244–249.

Conrad, D. L. *The Grants Planner*. San Francisco: Institute for Fund-Raising, 1976.

Conrad, D. L. *Successful Fund Raising Techniques*. San Francisco: Institute for Fund-Raising, 1977.

Glass, S. A. "A Winning Strategy." *CASE Currents*, May 1980, *6* (5), 29–31.

Hallahan, K. M. "Beirne Foundation: The Untold Story of the Labor Movement." *Foundation News*, November/December 1979, *20* (6), 21–24, 43–44.

Hartman, L., Mundel, J., and Shakely, J. "How a Foundation Makes a Grant." *Grantsmanship Center News*, August/September 1974, *1* (7), 1, 16–18.

Hillman, H. *The Art of Winning Corporate Grants*. New York: Vanguard Press, 1980.

Kurzig, C. M. *Foundation Fundamentals: A Guide for Grantseekers*. New York: The Foundation Center, 1980.

Lefferts, R. *Getting a Grant*. Englewood Cliffs, N.J.: Prentice-Hall, 1978.

Malo, P. "The Big Search." *Grantsmanship Center News*, October/December 1977, *3* (6), 35–40.

Mayor, R. A. "What Will a Foundation Look for When You Submit a Grant Proposal?" New York: The Foundation Center, 1972.

Saasta, T. "How Foundations Review Proposals and Make Grants." *Grantsmanship Center News*, November/December 1976, *3* (2), 9–19.

Saasta, T. "A Family of Family Foundations." *Grantsmanship Center News*, April/June 1977a, *3* (4), 24–29.

Saasta, T. "How the Ford Foundation Determines What (and Whom) It Will Support." *Grantsmanship Center News*. January/March 1977b, *3* (3), 9–18.

Warm, H. "How Grantseekers Lower the Odds." *Foundation News*. July/August 1979, *20* (4), 20–21, 37–39, 43.

John H. Buskey is associate dean of continuing studies and assistant professor of adult and continuing education at the University of Nebraska-Lincoln.

There are no promises, only premises
to float with,
words, words,
generated and disseminated, collated and bound;
versions of
ways to get, ways to receive, money
from the feds, forms for
the state (Mindell, 1980).

Project Management
and Operation

Lynn H. Willett

When an organization accepts a grant or contract from a funding agency it, in fact, has created a new and temporary organization (Miles, 1964). Membership in this organization is temporary for both the clients and the staff. The conditions of staff impermanence and short timelines create management problems for the project manager in: (1) planning for the award, (2) organizing staff and resources; (3) coordinating the new temporary organization with the existing permanent organization; and (4) phasing out the project and preparing for future audits.

Planning

Upon notification of the award from the agency or foundation, the first step is to complete the final negotiations. During this phase, the project director or grants officer must clearly establish the amount of the award, final budget revisions, and final project expectations. The method of payment should also be clearly established. Most federal and state agencies will pay in one of three ways: letter of credit, treasury advancement, or reimbursement. In contract negotiations, this process is highly formalized and well-documented. For grants from state, federal, or private agencies, this final negotiation may be unstructured and leave a number of

J. Buskey (Ed.). *New Directions for Continuing Education: Attracting External Funds for Continuing Education,* no. 12. San Francisco: Jossey-Bass, December 1981.

questions unanswered. Typical questions which should be asked at this time are:

- What restrictions exist on the use of funds?
- When do reports have to be submitted?
- Who owns the equipment?
- Can out-of-state travel be authorized?
- What project evaluation requirements are needed?
- What are the in-kind or matching dollar commitments?

Answers to these questions will help the project director specify what is expected of the organization.

Once a final award document has been received from the funding agency, the process of organizational sensitization should begin for the permanent staff, the governing board, and local community. This sensitization should utilize formal news releases explaining what the grant means to the organization, informal person-to-person discussions on the project, and small group meetings with significant service or support groups whose assistance will be needed. Additionally, the project director should follow internal reporting protocol by setting up the proper budget and accounting procedures, by securing project space and by obtaining the necessary physical resources such as filing cabinets, desks, telephones, and staff name cards.

Another important task which must be accomplished during the planning phase is to review thoroughly the funding agency's rules and regulations and required assurances. Regulations for federal grants are contained in various circulars prepared and supervised by the U.S. Office of Management and Budget (OMB). Circulars highly relevant to the management of continuing education projects are OMB Circulars No. A-102 and A-110 dealing with uniform administrative requirements, and Circulars No. A-21, A-87, and A-122 dealing with cost principles. See the chapter on federal regulations for detailed information on these circulars.

When organizations accept federal and state awards, they also are required to assure the government agency, in writing, that they will abide by certain laws and regulations. The more common assurances involve nondiscrimination on the basis of race, color, national origin, sex, handicap, or age, and safeguarding the rights and welfare of human subjects. Adherence to these requirements will insure that the project is conducted legally. Additional information about the assurances appears in Matelski's chapter on federal regulations.

Lastly, the organization's project director and grants/contracts officer should carefully review the entire grant. The funding agency's review process most likely has taken four to six months and interim changes in the permanent organization may have created changes in how the grant will be carried out. During this phase, the original project timelines should be revised and updated. Most likely the original deadlines were too ambitious and were based on an outdated start time. Once this final refinement phase of the grant is completed, the next phase of organization can begin smoothly.

Organizing

In his analysis of temporary organizations, Miles found that staff working in temporary organizations are operating under more stress than their "permanent" colleagues (1964, p. 457). This stress tends to narrow the staff's time perspective. The staff person becomes focused on the present and neglects plans for the future. Effective project organization should acknowledge this fact and designate appropriate strategies which insure that project activities will be carried out systematically through adequate staffing, project refinement, and detailed recordkeeping.

The recruitment of staff becomes one of the first priorities the project director faces. If new staff are recruited, this process must be in conformance with the regulations of the agency which provided the funds. If staff are being assigned (either full- or part-time) from within the organization, this shift of load and the specific time commitments and compensation should be clearly spelled out in job descriptions. Copies of memos and recruiting letters become a part of the temporary organization's project file.

Once the project director and new staff are oriented to the task, a detailed internal planning effort should be conducted. For each of the project objectives, step-by-step procedures should be spelled out. These procedures should answer the questions of who, what, when, where, and how the activities will be accomplished. A useful method for formatting this process is shown in Figure 1. A second step to this planning effort is the designation of project *milestones*. Milestones are the important accomplishments which must be achieved if the project is to be successful, and which must be completed within the time frame of the grant. In a personnel hiring process, a variety of activities are conducted ranging from writing a job description to conducting interviews. The milestone, however, is the appointment and acceptance of the newly hired staff person. Establishing milestones is an important strategy for helping staff in temporary organizations reduce stress, provide immediate time orientation and provide opportunities for recognition of accomplishment.

Next, staff should get involved in developing appropriate forms for use in the project. Most continuing education projects will involve working with clients, and data on these people must be collected. The usual demographic variables of age, sex, education, residence, and similar items will be a part of the client form. Other forms which need to be developed at the start of the project could include: an anecdotal report form for staff on indirect project outcomes, part-time payroll sheets, client feedback checklists and staff time-logs. Keeping each of these forms in a separate three-

Figure 1. Management Action Plan

Objective Statement:

Tasks	Starting Date	Ending Date	Responsible Person	Milestone
1.	1.	1.	1.	1.
2.	2.	2.	2.	2.
3.	3.	3.	3.	3.

ring notebook provides an effective method for organizing and maintaining the ongoing project data bank.

Official financial records must be kept with the agency's treasurer or comptroller. However, most temporary organizations because of their transitory nature, tight timelines and unusual external agency requirements, should set up their own separate accounting records tailored to the needs of the specific project. These separate records will give the project director accurate and immediate data on where the project stands in relation to the expenditure of grant funds, the allocation of matching funds, and the transfer of indirect cost monies.

Shown in Figure 2 is a form developed by University of Nebraska staff for recording accounting information (Buskey, 1980). Individual columns are provided for each major expenditure category of the project's budget, as well as for the date, number, and description of each requisition. To demonstrate the use of the form (normally 8½″ x 11″ size), the budget shown in the *Amount Requested* column in Figure 1 in Willett's chapter on project budgeting has been used; a similar set of records should be maintained for the matching funds. To use the system, record the approved budget amounts by category (as detailed as needed) in the columns on the first line; this provides an instant basis for later comparison. Record each item of expenditure, for example, requisitions, payroll records, travel vouchers, *as soon as a document is initiated;* this will provide a chronological list of expenditures. At the end of each month, or at any other convenient time, the project director can calculate a subtotal and quickly find out the state of the entire budget. In permanent organizations which conduct many projects, standard blank forms can be produced and column headings appropriate to specific projects can be easily typed in.

Continuing education projects in colleges and universities can quickly get in trouble because the large permanent system may be slow in providing temporary organization financial status reports. The project staff should periodically reconcile their financial records, such as those

Figure 2. Accounting Information Form

Req. #	Date	Description	Staff Salaries	Benefits	Contr. Svcs.	Non-Personnel Costs	Indirect Costs	TOTAL
-	7/1/81	Budget	$34,800	$6,646	$18,580	$2,710	$5,018	$67,754
1	7/3/81	Typew. Rental				64		64
2	7/6/81	Eval. Consult.			100	10		110
-	7/31/81	July Total	0	0	100	74	0	174
3	8/3/81	Salaries-July	2,900	554				3,454

described above, with the official records maintained by the permanent organization. Financial records which must be maintained by the organization are copies of requisitions, purchase orders, equipment specifications, bid announcements, payroll sheets, personnel contracts, employee fringe benefits paperwork, and travel vouchers.

Project staff, after developing the detailed management plan, should construct their own monitoring forms and establish their own financial records. This activity will alleviate the problems associated with narrow time perspectives often found in temporary organizations. Once these activities are accomplished, the staff embarks on the day-to-day task of coordinating the project.

Coordination

One of the common problems in temporary organizations is that communication with the external permanent organization—and in some cases with the funding agency—is far less effective than within the tightly knit group. A tendency exists for the small temporary staff to become a closed communication system as they focus on accomplishing the project's objectives and tasks. An essential ingredient in effective continuing education project coordination is to establish effective and frequent communications with the various organizational units which can supply service, manpower, and resources to the temporary organization. The areas of external communication, formative evaluation, interim reporting, and budget monitoring are at the heart of effective project management.

Maintaining effective external communication links with the permanent organization will solidify cooperative efforts. During the life of the continuing education project, it is easy for the staff in the permanent organization to ignore, discount, or reject the temporary organization's efforts. The project staff must develop external communication via newsletters, memos, status reports and informal one-on-one personal relationships with external key staff. Another effective device for gaining external collaboration is to utilize personnel from the permanent organization as consultants, curriculum developers, evaluators, or advisory committee people. Providing these staff with small stipends quickly creates a base of support which would not exist otherwise.

Most funded continuing education projects have an evaluation strategy as part of the overall design. Formative, or ongoing, evaluation is an effective strategy for project staff to assess how the project is progressing. On the basis of periodic assessments, adjustments can be made during the project to insure project success. Formative evaluation should involve, at a minimum, assessment by the temporary organization staff of a sample of the clients being served by the project, review of the anecdotal records being collected, evaluation of informal feedback from external key staff, and an intensive and frank assessment of progress toward accomplishing the milestones identified in the planning phases of the project. All of these sources of feedback on the project become a rich resource for writing interim project status reports.

Most funding agencies require grant or contract recipients to submit at least one interim progress report; often, quarterly reports are required. The purpose of these reports is to provide the funding agency with a formal assessment of where the project is going. In some cases, if serious problems exist, the agency may make a site visit to review with the project staff problems which are hindering the progress of the project. Interim progress reports are an excellent opportunity for the temporary organization staff to synthesize their formative evaluation data and also to redirect the project toward more productive directions. An element of most interim reports is a report on the expenditure of money.

The temporary organization's budget expenditures should be reconciled with the permanent organization's data every month. The project staff should make a concrete determination of where the budget stands. By the end of the second or third quarter, budget problems typically exist in three areas: (1) personnel line-items are generally underspent because many staff were brought into the temporary organization after the official start date; (2) supply line-items are usually dangerously close to being overspent because most budget makers tend to underestimate this line-item; and (3) contractual services will probably be underspent because the consultant has not yet been called in and a third party summative evaluation has not been conducted. Travel expenditures at midyear are generally on target.

Another ancillary budget problem encountered during the coordination phase is the cash flow problem. In smaller organizations, the flow of money from the funding agency to the temporary organization creates problems of cash flow. Cash flow problems exist when authorized expenditures are being made but the authorized money from the funding source has not arrived. Organizations which anticipate that cash flow may be a problem need to advocate a frequent and predictable pay-out schedule from the funding agency. Responding to the various coordination challenges through effective communication, evaluation, and reporting brings the project into synchronization with the agency's requirements. Project staff can now begin the all-important task of completing the program and phasing out the temporary organization.

Termination

Research on temporary organizations shows that most projects suffer from a slow startup and low initial productivity (Miles, 1964). As the project nears completion, high staff productivity exists and large numbers of concrete results are produced in a short period. A problem which may confound this typical work cycle is the early departure of the key staff members. Because some of the staff may not have a "hard-money" position readily available, they may expend their energies on finding another job. As the project winds down, data must be organized for final reporting. The summative evaluation must be planned, conducted, and written. Accurate projections on final budget expenditures must be done sixty days prior to the end of the project. In some cases, overexpenditure of line-items may have occurred. Most federal and state agencies allow up to 10 percent line-item expenditure deviation without formal written approval; however, this 10 percent margin is not allowed for the final project total. If overexpenditure is occurring in one line-item, corresponding underexpenditure must occur in other areas of the budget. Project staff should ascertain from the funding agency the exact percentage of over or underexpenditure that can be allowed without the agency's approval.

Staff also need to develop an action plan for producing the final project written report. All agencies require end-of-project reporting. Generally, this report includes specific auditable data on what the project accomplished in numbers of persons or agencies served, characteristics of those served, and measurable outcomes of the service performed. Also, a narrative description of the overall conduct of the project from the perspective of the staff is important. Generally appended to this description is a third party evaluation. Most federal and state agencies require that the end of project report be submitted within 90 days.

While the staff's preoccupation is with communicating the project's outcomes to the funding agency, consideration also should be given to providing some of these data to internal institutional audiences. This feedback, in short, summary form, is an effective device for maintaining relationships with supportive groups as well as educating the project critics.

In some cases, continuing education projects do not finish on schedule. This is due to a wide range of variables: late start, staff turnover, shift in target population, unproductive subcontractual relationships, and so forth. If the temporary organization foresees that the project cannot be completed on time, a telephone call to the agency, followed up by a written request, may result in an extension of the final ending date. If an extension is granted, the project director will have to insure that enough project funds exist to accommodate the extension. Most agency extensions are not accompanied by a corresponding increase in project funding.

After the final report is submitted, the last task of the project staff is to establish permanent files for the project. Agencies generally establish requirements that project records must be available for a certain period of time following project completion. This period can vary from one year to seven years. The final project records must be organized so that permanent agency staff and funding agency auditors can systematically review the project long after the temporary organization staff has left.

An exciting and generally productive post-project activity is a six or twelve month follow-up of the project. Some of the most concrete project results surface after the program has been completed. If the permanent organization can provide funds for conducting this activity, the funding agency will be most impressed to receive this feedback. This postproject evaluation can become an effective mechanism for gaining new funds to support other continuing education projects.

Summary

The temporary organization offers an excellent organizational background perspective from which the management action, procedures, and processes of an externally funded continuing education project can be conducted. Research on the temporary organization provides a valuable insight into the complex pressures which exist in accomplishing the contract or grant objectives.

An efficient and well-organized project management operation ensures success for the current project. A successfully managed project may also be the springboard to other funding from that agency or may impress the permanent administration so that the project will be continued within the permanent organization.

References and Further Readings

Argyris, C. *Management and Organizational Development: The Path from XA to YB*. New York: McGraw-Hill, 1971.

Borst, D. and Montana, P. *Managing Nonprofit Organizations*. New York: AMACON, Division of American Management Associations, 1977.

[Buskey, J. H.] "Guidelines for Budgeting Programs Conducted by Learning Centers." Lincoln, Neb.: Division of Continuing Studies, University of Nebraska-Lincoln, 1980.

Cook, D. L. *Educational Project Management*. Columbus, Ohio: Charles Merrill, 1971.

"Education Division General Administrative Regulations (EDGAR)." *Federal Register*, April 3, 1980, *45* (66), 22494–22631. Washington, D.C.: U.S. Department of Health, Education, and Welfare, Education Division, 1980.

Federal Grants Management Handbook. Washington, D.C.: Grants Management Advisory Service, 1981.

Hendricks, W. *Grants Administration*. Arlington, Va.: National Graduate University, 1972.

Krebs, R. E. *Grants and Contracts Handbook*. Park Forest South, Ill.: Governors State University, 1975.

Leslie, J. W. "A Resource Allocation Information System: For Managing an Institutional Advancement Program." *College and University Journal*, May, 1973 *12* (3), 19–21, 27–29.

Miles, M. B. "On Temporary Systems." In M. B. Miles (Ed.), *Innovation in Education*. New York: Teacher's College Press, Columbia University, 1964.

Mindell, D. "The Grantswriter." Unpublished poem. Elgin, Ill.: Elgin Community College, July 28, 1980.

U.S. Office of Management and Budget. *Catalog of Federal Domestic Assistance*. Washington, D.C.: U.S. Government Printing Office, 1980.

Zaltman, G. (Ed.). *Management Principles for Nonprofit Agencies and Organizations*. New York: AMACON, Division of American Management Associations, 1979.

Lynn H. Willett is vice president for development and community services at Elgin Community College in Elgin, Illinois, and for ten years has been involved in resource development as a grantsman, teacher and writer.

*Input through education anticipates a multiplied
output which is reflected in social and economic
benefit to the society. Investment in education
assumes a multiplier effect on the input such that the
output is greater than the initial expenditure, but
outcomes are the real measure used by society.*

The Multiplier Effect

William L. Flowers, Jr.
John B. Harris

The multiplier effect is a phenomenon of change best exemplified in nature. The multiplier effect either helps or inhibits the advancement of humankind or its use of resources. In this chapter, the multiplier is about people teaching people with a focus on people as application-users of knowledge. In order to achieve ongoing adult development, there must be money for those in continuing education to achieve their goals. The thesis in this chapter is that as one idea leads to another, so one grant may lead to another. Simply put, the multiplier effect is a quantity which is added to the original. The multiplier effect represents productive growth and is linked, in this chapter, to attracting external dollars for continuing education programs. Because quantitative change is also related to qualitative change (Hegeland, 1966), there is pedagogical value in examining the multiplier effect. Ideally, an educational multiplier effect is applied to improvement of the human condition (Pinnock, 1979). The most frequently used common denominator in the American society is dollar economics. So, ultimately, the multiplier effect relates to the bottom line—income generation. Reduced to a formula we get: continuing education $\times$ application = growth/progress/increase.

The concept of the multiplier effect is not new, although application to continuing education is recent (Brown, 1981). This multiplier effect represents dynamic growth (characterized by continuing education) as con-

J. Buskey (Ed.). *New Directions for Continuing Education: Attracting External Funds
for Continuing Education,* no. 12. San Francisco: Jossey-Bass, December 1981.

trasted with the status quo, a static state, or slow change experienced among many colleges working in traditional (though important) campus programs.

Arithmetically, we know that when one factor is multiplied by another the expected outcome is that the multiplied object increases. The key concept is increase. But, an arithmetical multiplier has exceptions which must be acknowledged in this analogy. First, the result is nothing if the multiplier is zero. Second, there is no increase if the multiplier is one. Third, there is a decrease if the multiplier is more than zero but less than one. Only a multiplier value greater than one will lead to an increase. Educational needs of adult users of continuing education can be similarly characterized.

Educational needs of the society overlap in such a way that when one need is met or removed, as with a shingle from a roof, at least two more needs are then more completely revealed. Human beings are curious, knowledge thirsty, developing organisms such that their perfect inventions lead to more perfect improvements and then, to still other improvements. A contemporary example is a decade of development in computer technology.

The nature of continuing education programs is such that the overlapping pattern of needs described above seems an appropriate description. While meeting adult educational needs, there is, concurrently, a discovery of additional educational needs—hence, the multiplier principle. When one need is met, other partially-met, new educational needs appear. So, the multiplier effect is in fact a part of the process of change. The problems of people represent opportunities for change. "Show me a nation and a people who have no problems and I will show you a nation and a people waiting to arrive in the twentieth century" (Pinnock, 1979, p. 56).

The Multiplier Effect and Continuing Education

In the field of continuing education, the application of the multiplier effect has been demonstrated in the case of the Kellogg centers for continuing education. As an early proponent of continuing education, W. K. Kellogg said, "I'll invest my money in people" ("A Biographical Sketch . . . ," 1980, p. 1). Extension and continuing education practitioners are sustaining that earlier concept and are employing a multiplier effect.

In 1936, the University of Minnesota opened its Center for Continuation Study with assistance from the federal government. In 1944, Michigan State University requested Kellogg Foundation support for an Extension Service Program which would bring young farmers to the University campus for programs suited to their agricultural knowledge needs. These courses also included public speaking, health, and nutrition. This program led to the concept of a separate university facility for the Rural Life Institute. Concurrently, the Hotel Association of Michigan cited a need for the University to teach courses in hotel administration. This combination of events led to the concept of a residential continuing education center (Mawby, 1979).

But this was only the nucleus of the idea. The initial multiplier effect came when the Kellogg Foundation in 1951 provided funds for the first residential center for continuing education at Michigan State University and later furnished partial assistance grants for nine additional centers. Since then, the multiplier effect has resulted in over 200 similar centers throughout the world (Mawby, 1979). In these continuing education centers, thousands of programs have been planned and presented. Tens of thousands of participants have logged hundreds of thousands of hours in instructional contact time. The multiplier effect has had a dramatic impact.

More than a decade ago, a management theory which originated on college and university campuses was applied in business and industry. It was called "management by objectives." This theory gained additional emphasis when some state governments and the federal government began to use the concept. Underlying this concept was the notion of how those in management could cause employees to increase or multiply their efforts. Extension education, continuing education, workshops, and sensitivity sessions were some of the activities employed to achieve this multiplier effect. The idea itself spread and, in the business world, its use has increased over and over again. Objectives of organizations and individuals were designed to be "quantifiable," "measurable." Even the U.S. Congress enacted legislation, such as the Food and Agricultural Act of 1977, which required that agencies document "the economic and social consequences" of their research and education programs (U.S. Congress, 1977). The Congress, along with business and industry, wanted evidence that there was or was not a multiplier effect of education on the economic well-being of citizens.

The Third User of Knowledge

If we consider a teacher as the first user of knowledge and the student of that teacher the second user, then the one who applies that knowledge is the third user of knowledge. The multiplier effect stops when knowledge invested through adult education programs exists in a passive state; knowledge is dormant in terms of results until applied by a user. Using the arithmetical examples cited above, this unapplied knowledge may have the same value as if it were multiplied by zero, by a factor less than one, or by one. The "demonstration method," employed domestically for less than a century by Cooperative Extension personnel and used by other adults for ages before that, has lately been redefined among persons who now "train the trainer." This technique is characterized by an implicit multiplier objective. The demonstrator or the trainer assumes a multiplier and, accordingly, develops handouts, notebooks, or other materials with that idea in mind. The emphasis is on training others who then will train still others.

A program to certify pesticide applicators in Virginia demonstrates the extent to which the third user of knowledge concept may be systematically and effectively employed for the benefit of people in their communities. A small group of people who were experts in the safe application of pesticides conducted a half dozen "train-the-trainer" sessions for approximately 160 Virginia extension agents and specialists, and they, in turn, trained approximately 38,000 individuals ("Virginia . . . ," 1975). Thus, a small group of experts (perhaps six in number), by training a larger group (160), ultimately had an educational impact on a very large number (38,000) of third users of knowledge. When one considers that the ratio of trainers in the first group to the users in the third group was one to 6,333, one realizes the dramatic power of the multiplier effect.

When the third user of knowledge shares that knowledge through application (via demonstrations or instruction) with still other users, the group which made the initial input may not recognize the extent of the expansion which takes place through sharing. In any case, the funding agency, the granting foundation, or the supporting business and industry can be more readily convinced to award subsequent grants if there are documented data on the changes that have taken place as a result of the initial support.

Several examples of the use of grants as means to multiply continuing education programs can be cited by experienced practitioners in the field. These can be related to or based on multiplier effect theories. Recognizing that few, if any, instructional plans satisfy all of the initially perceived needs, application of the multiplier concept in continuing education has been employed to: (1) refine programs or expand services, (2) enhance staff competence and develop the organization's capability, (3) provide the basis for attracting other grants or support, and (4) develop a track record of accountability in the use and application of continuing education resources.

External Funds and Organizational Mission

Efficient use of resources is a focus for most professional practitioners concerned with application of knowledge through continuing education. Program planners look naturally to available financial resources to support programming for audiences who need to apply knowledge. Grants and contracts (or "soft money") from federal, state, and private agencies have become common sources of extra funding to supplement the traditional "hard money" resources of fee income and tax sources. In a chapter titled "Soft Money and Hard Facts: Grants and Contracts in the Overall Plan," Elinor Lenz discusses the realities of budget and ethics associated with using contracts, grants and other external funds for continuing education programming. She points out, for example, that organizations must be sensitive to the balance between their external funding and their basic budget and how these two (or more) sources of funds interact with each other. The ethical issues focus on the extent to which external funding from a donor may alter the mission of the educational enterprise and possibly compromise objectivity and integrity (Lenz, 1980). These are crucial issues that may well determine the long-range success of the organization.

Grants represent soft money, and productive instruction for the application-motivated enrollee determines whether there will be multiplied participation by the adult consumer of education. The bottom line for the consumer becomes, "What was in it for me?" A positive response to self assessment of program value encourages the former adult program participant to become a future enrollee. For the adult education programmer, those so motivated represent "repeat business," a multiplier effect. This builds confidence in program effectiveness which makes it easier for continuing education program planners to attract grants or other forms of support resources.

Summary

The funding base of many successful externally supported programs has been enhanced and expanded by soft money received by using the multiplier effect. Documenting cause and effect through continuing education programs are basic elements in establishing a track record of productivity with prior grants. The same business accountability philosophies which developed huge fortunes and enabled the establishment of granting foundations also guides many granting governmental agencies. Those who run foundations, as those who run government granting agencies, look for the potential multiplier effect. All expect programs to produce an output greater than the input.

Implicit in program support concern is a comprehensively conceived evaluation plan considering multiple influence on single clients or client clusters. Documenting cause and effect of granted resources directed towards target audiences may be obtained by appropriate follow up. Relatively little of this is done beyond a fiscal year or grant period, but it is the material from which new projects are developed. And without it, there may

94

be a multiplier effect arithmetically characterized as if the multiplier were one, less than one, or zero.

References

"A Biographical Sketch of the Founder of the Kellogg Company and the W. K. Kellogg Foundation." *Kellogg Foundation.* Battle Creek, Michigan: W. K. Kellogg Foundation, 1980.

Brown, B. "Spotlight Interview: A Conversation with John H. Buskey." *Funding Review,* April/June 1981, *1* (3), 6–9, 46–48.

Hegeland, H. *The Multiplier Theory.* New York: A. M. Kelly Publishers, 1966.

Lenz, E. *Creating and Marketing Programs in Continuing Education.* New York: McGraw-Hill, 1980.

Mawby, R. G., and others. *W. K. Kellogg Foundation, The First Half Century: Private Approaches to Public Needs.* Battle Creek, Mich.: W. K. Kellogg Foundation, 1979.

Pinnock, T. J. *Tuskegee Institute and the New Leaders of the Rural South— Partners in an Evolutionary Process: Annual Report.* Tuskegee, Ala.: Tuskegee Institute, 1979.

U.S. Congress. *Food and Agricultural Act of 1977,* Section 1459, Title XIV, 1977.

"Virginia State Plan for Certification of Pesticide Applicators." *Exhibit B, Plans for Pesticide Application Training,* M. F. Ellmore (training coordinator). Blacksburg, Va., July 14, 1975.

William L. Flowers, Jr., is professor and associate dean of the Extension Division at Virginia Polytechnic Institute and State University, Blacksburg, Virginia. He has worked for over thirty years in the field of human development and has specialized in using the multiplier effect to bring about social and economic change in rural areas through generating program support including the acquisition of foundation and governmental resources.

John B. Harris is associate professor of business at Virginia State University at Petersburg, director of the Virginia State Office of Minority Business Enterprise, and a special assistant to the governor of Virginia for minority enterprise. He is a writer, consultant, marketing specialist and researcher, and his experience includes the academic, private, and public service sectors.

*Contracting is an untapped resource for continuing
education administrators in which competition is
vigorous but the financial rewards are worthwhile.*

Contracting

Frank G. Adams

Contracting, a world previously reserved for university researchers and
private corporations, has become an important funding source for continuing education administrators, most of whom work in nonprofit organizations. Because contracts are open to profit and nonprofit organizations, the
administrator must be able to project costs within a slight margin of error
in order to be competitive. The advantage the administrator has over
profit-making organizations is the talent pool available from the institution. More than half the private contractors rely on personnel from college
and university campuses or community-based organizations for the talent
necessary to carry out the contract.

Grants and Contracts: The Differences

The differences between grants and contracts are many but none of
the characteristics of a contract is so unique that it prohibits the administrator from participating in the bidding process. In general, the administrator who has written grant proposals will be able to adjust to the contracting process quite easily.

Specifications. Grants are used to transfer money, property, services,
or anything of value to a recipient to accomplish a public purpose of
support or stimulation. Specifications for federal grants are determined
through legislation which is then communicated to potential grantees

J. Buskey (Ed.). *New Directions for Continuing Education: Attracting External Funds
for Continuing Education,* no. 12. San Francisco: Jossey-Bass, December 1981.

through the *Federal Register,* a daily publication of federal regulations. The regulations are related to legislative goals established by statute. The administrator is permitted to address priorities from the context of local needs. Grant objectives, the program to carry out the objectives, and the method for evaluating the outcomes are primarily left to the proposal writer.

Contracts are a means for the federal government to purchase a specific service or product, such as educational materials, personnel training, buildings, or evaluation of granted programs. Well over 50 percent of contracts relate to some form of technical services such as training, evaluation, or research. Contract specifications are *not* related to specific legislation but to specific tasks to be accomplished by a federal agency. Therefore, the agency seeks the best value for the federal government. This is why both profit and nonprofit agencies may bid for a contract.

A summary list of contrasting specifications is listed in Figure 1 to more succinctly illustrate pertinent differences between grants and contracts.

Eligibility. Grant announcements tend to specify the kinds of organizations to which grants will be made. They will almost always be to some type of nonprofit institution or agency, and, in many cases, the grants are made from a federal government agency to a state or local government entity. This process eliminates many other potential grantees.

Ideally, contracts offer the best quality for the most reasonable price to the government. Federal agencies are less concerned about the type of institution or agency offering a bid as long as it follows the appropriate criteria. The criteria for some contracts require that the award go to a specific kind of organization such as a minority- or woman-owned business, or a small business. In some cases the entire solicitation is set aside for minority or small businesses. The rule for qualifying as a small business is determined by the Small Business Administration of the U.S. Department of Commerce. A small business eligibility qualification for one solicitation does not mean the institution or corporation will necessarily qualify for small business standing on another proposal.

Methods of Procurement and Types of Contracts

The federal government uses two basic methods of procurement when it needs to purchase goods or services. The first is called *formal advertising* and is characterized by the issuance of an invitation for bids (IFB). The second method is called a *negotiated procurement* and a request for proposals (RFP) is issued. In essence, these two terms define a continuum of procurement methodology which enables the government to act flexibly within prescribed rules.

Figure 1. Differences Between Grants and Contracts

Grant	*Contract*
1. Allows writer to select programs	1. Describes very specific tasks or groups to be served
2. Requires elaborately defined objectives, procedures, and evaluation	2. Requires completion of a specific set of tasks
3. Requires elaborate, specific budgets	3. Requires a cost breakdown
4. Requires general accountability for expenditures and record keeping	4. Requires rigid accountability of cost accounting
5. Has a tendency toward lengthy proposal and elaborate backup materials	5. Most contract bids are put together by the agency with the bidder responding in 10–20 pages of concise statements specific to the tasks
6. Describes an outcome that may be a "best estimate" or probable result	6. Requires a specific outcome
7. Bases monitoring regulations on appropriateness to nonprofit organizations	7. Bases monitoring regulations on federal procurement procedures which are different from grant regulations
8. Numerous grant awards are made as a result of one announcement	8. One bidder usually receives the entire award
9. Has submission deadline that is usually 60–90 days or longer after announcement or *Federal Register* publication	9. Has submission deadline that is usually 21–45 days after announcement
10. Allows grantee to determine the location for the program	10. The contracting agency determines time, date, and location of the program
11. Grantee may receive an indirect cost rate to cover administration of the program	11. Since the contractor is offering the best price to the government the federal agency looks for fairness— not a fixed administration cost. In many cases the bidder will also be permitted a fee

There are also two primary types of contracts awarded as a result of the two procurement methods identified above. The IFB usually results in issuance of a firm-fixed-price contract, while the RFP often results in the award of a cost reimbursement contract. These procurement methods, types of contracts, and their interrelationships are described in detail in Matelski's chapter on federal regulations.

It should be noted that one of the options available to contract officers is the sole source procurement in which the government seeks a single supplier or contractor. This type of procurement occurs about 20 to 30 percent of the time and is common when a bidding contractor has satisfactorily completed a contract but the government wants to continue the program or have the contractor add to the effort through a new contract. An example of this arrangement may occur when a continuing educator has provided training for one office in an agency through a bid process and another office wants the same training.

Who Wins the Contracts?

There are two facts to reiterate here. First, contracts can be more lucrative than grants. Second, solicitations for bids allow both profit and nonprofit agencies to participate. Contracts are definitely competitive. Profit-making consulting and training firms have sprung up all across the nation to take part in this activity. They have a skilled staff. They understand cost accounting procedures, and they are willing to spend the time to draft superbly written proposals. There are colleges and universities with long-standing records of research contracting which are also active. Few continuing education administrators, however, make the attempt even though they are located near major federal installations or federal regional offices which issue contract solicitations.

In the private sector, many large contractors maintain well-staffed offices in Washington or in major cities where federal regional offices are located. However, institutionally based continuing education administrators have as much opportunity to bid successfully as the most sophisticated private firms. One advantage lies in the fact that the administrator has an expertise pool through which research, training, or consulting to federal agencies could be provided with little difficulty since the expert is associated with the institution.

What many continuing education administrators lack is the bidding expertise to win contracts. These are skills that can be learned in a short time through practice or through one of the many seminars and workshops held around the country. The long years of experience acquired by private companies will still create keen competition. The private companies bidding on contracts for training, research, and consulting often employ faculty and staff from school districts, colleges and universities as private consultants to provide the expertise necessary to respond to a specific contract opportunity. Thus, continuing education administrators lose the revenue they could gain by tapping into their own talent pool.

Who Issues Contract Solicitations and for What?

Continuing education administrators will tend to be most interested in training contracts although federal agencies will frequently request consulting services or research. The range of solicitations is so broad that there could easily be something of interest for all continuing educators. A six-month analysis of the *Commerce Business Daily* from November 1980 through April, 1981 reveals no less than 322 separate requests for proposals that might be of interest to continuing education administrators. A few examples are cited in Figure 2 as illustrations of the variety of opportunities available.

The examples in Figure 2 represent only a tiny fraction of the courses, seminars, workshops, and technical training requested over a six-month period. The requests indicated in the sample range in price from a few thousand dollars to over $2,000,000. A similar analysis of requests for expert and consultant services and research indicated an equal number of requests for training.

Over a twelve-month period, even the novice administrator should discover at least twenty to thirty opportunities to compete for contracts that are within the parameters of the institution's goals.

Understanding the Process

Though writing proposals for contracts is actually easier than writing proposals for grants, administrators who receive RFPs do not always view them seriously. This is because many RFPs are written in legal terms and cite unfamiliar procurement regulations. The format is so different from the grant proposal that most contract RFPs are disregarded.

It is quite simple for the administrator to begin bidding on contracts. With two documents and some writing talent, a staff can be on its way to a new venture and new alternatives for continuing education services.

The first document needed is the *Commerce Business Daily*, which contains, in brief form, the information necessary to know who is soliciting a contract, what it is for, and how to get copies of the bid proposal.

The second document needed is the *Bidder's Mailing List Application* which is Government Standard Form 129. Forms are readily available through any Small Business Administration office. This application permits the institution to be placed on the various government direct mail lists, if the agency keeps a mailing list. In this way the administrator is assured RFPs will come to the office directly should they be missed in the *Commerce Business Daily*.

Assuming the institution has an attorney who can interpret the legal language of contracts, the administrator is on the way to preparing bid proposals.

Unique Characteristics of Contracts

The contracting business has its own jargon. Sometimes solicitations and contract documents are confusing because occasionally federal

Figure 2. Contract Solicitations

Source of Request	Nature of Request
U.S. Army	Basic Academic Skills (five RFPs)
Environmental Protection Agency	Management Skills Training
Forest Service	Management Skills Training
Power Administration	Equal Opportunity Training
Housing and Urban Development	Consumer Economics Training
U.S. Army	Operation of an On-Post Learning Resource Center
U.S. Navy	Technical Office Skills
U.S. Navy	College Classes Aboard Ship
Bureau of Indian Affairs	Supervisory Skills Training
Veteran's Administration	Communication Skills Training
U.S. Army	Foreign Language Courses
State Department	Supervisory Skills Training

agencies will modify the solicitation and issue addenda, or "change notices" altering the due dates, wording, or contact persons. These are contracts and the government holds itself and the contractor more accountable for exact wording of the document than it does in a grant. Rarely does a grantee sue the government for violation of the terms of a grant. Conversely, the government may be sued for costs incurred by a contractor. Therefore, the contracting nomenclature tends to be more precise.

Some solicitations are titled RFPs (request for proposal). The RFP requires the potential contractor to provide both a pricing proposal and a narrative or technical statement of how the tasks of the contract are to be carried out. The pricing proposal is a cost breakdown of how the bidder arrived at the costs. In issuing an RFP the agency has already determined a range of costs acceptable to the government. The best proposal falling within the range is likely to get the contract.

Another common abbreviation is the RFQ (request for quotation). The RFQ is usually an indication that the federal agency has not determined a range of costs or has not previously solicited for a similar contract. In this case once an RFQ has been responded to, the government may come back to the bidder for a full proposal based on the quotation. The RFQ is a very rough price estimate.

Sometimes an agency may use the term RFA (request for application). The RFA is most often used with grants but from time to time shows up in contracts. When the RFA is requested, the agency is generally seeking a more elaborate technical plan than an RFP asks for.

In all cases, the solicitation will have one or more contact persons indicated. If there is any doubt about the nature or intent of the solicitation, call the contact person to clarify the situation. Do this in advance. Once the submission deadline has passed, it is difficult to get amendments added to your bid.

Patterns in the Solicitation Process

There are certain patterns to watch for in the contracting process. For instance, many RFPs of interest to continuing education administrators will come in the last quarter of the federal fiscal year. Watching the *Commerce Business Daily* from April through June will provide many opportunities for short term training contracts. Agencies will tend to solicit at the end of the fiscal year while the funds are available.

About 10 to 20 percent of the contracts will not be awarded. This will usually happen because the federal agency received bids that are all in excess of the funds available. In other words, the agency's estimate of the bid price was too low.

Summary

The contracting process offers a unique funding source for continuing education administrators. Diligence in selecting contracts to bid, sticking close to home, and developing good relationships with the agencies with whom contracts are sought are the real keys to success.

The differences between grants and contracts are essential to understanding the benefits to be derived from contracts. The differences, or newness of the concept, should not be a deterrent to participation in the contract bidding process. Obviously, with the number of private firms actively engaged in contract bidding, the process must be manageable and financially worth the effort.

As continuing education budgets become tighter in the next decade, contracting services may be a new funding option for continuing education administrators to explore. It appears that government grants and contracts, industrial business contracts, and institutional resources will need to be packaged carefully to maintain effective continuing education programs in the 1980s.

References and Resources

Baker, K. "The New Contractsmanship." *The Grantsmanship Center News*, March/April 1976, *2* (7) (Issue 15), 21–61.
Bidder's Mailing List Application, Standard Form 129, U.S. Department of Commerce, Small Business Administration.

102

"Cost Principles for Educational Institutions." (OMB Circular No. A-21) *Federal Register,* March 6, 1979, *44* (45). Washington, D.C.: Office of Management and Budget, 1979.

Federal Grants and Contracts Weekly. Arlington, Va.: Capitol Publications, weekly publication.

Procurement Mailing List. Chicago, Ill.: U.S. General Services Administration, 1979.

U.S. Department of Commerce. *Commerce Business Daily.* Washington, D.C.: U.S. Government Printing Office, daily publication.

U.S. Department of Commerce. *Federal Register.* Washington, D.C.: U.S. Government Printing Office, daily publication.

University Resources, 425 East 58th Street, New York, N.Y.

Frank G. Adams is dean of open campus at the College of Lake County and is President of Educational Resources Institute. In the past five years he has been involved in raising more than $10,000,000 for continuing education programs for the college. Additionally, he conducts grants and contracts seminars through the Bureau of Business and Technology, New York.

There's no such thing as a free lunch!

Federal Regulations

Stanley M. Matelski

The federal legislative process that has developed since the founding of the United States is indeed complex. The continuing education administrator who desires involvement with government contracts and grants should have at least a cursory understanding of those parts of the process that directly affect the establishment, funding, and regulation of federally sponsored programs.

Legislative Process

The framers of the United States Constitution embodied in our system of government the principle of "separation of powers" by establishing three independent and equal branches of government—the legislative, the executive, and the judicial. The first provision of the Constitution (Article I, Section I) creates the legislative branch by establishing the Congress of the United States. Article I, Section 9 then gives the Congress control over federal financial affairs by prohibiting payments from the Treasury unless Congress has appropriated funds. The Anti-Deficiency Act of 1870 implements this power. In part:

> No officer or employee of the United States shall make or authorize an expenditure from or create or authorize an obligation under any appropriation or fund in excess of the amount available

J. Buskey (Ed.). *New Directions for Continuing Education: Attracting External Funds for Continuing Education,* no. 12. San Francisco: Jossey-Bass, December 1981.

therein; nor shall any such officer or employee involve the government in any contract or other obligation, for the payment of money for any purpose, in advance of appropriations made for such purpose, unless such contract or obligation is authorized by law.

Authorization. Congress first passes an authorization act. This authorizing measure is a public law with one or several objectives: to establish a federal agency, prescribe certain activities, or direct performance of some action. Authorizing legislation may be silent on the matter of funding for such activities, may authorize such sums as may be necessary, or may authorize funds not to exceed specific amounts. Except for general guidance or establishing a funding ceiling, the authorization act has no direct fiscal effect, for the authorizing measure cannot itself appropriate funds.

Appropriation. Congress then appropriates funds through separate acts for those activities authorized in previous legislation; appropriated funds may only be spent for those specified activities. This affords Congress a method through which it may exercise varying degrees of control over the activities or programs by the specificity of language used in designating such activities and programs.

Even though activities are authorized, Congress may delay or refuse appropriations. If an amount is specified in an authorization act, it may well be subject to drastic downward revision upon appropriation.

Other Actions. Once an appropriation of funds has been made by Congress, then the executive branch of the government, through the Office of Management and Budget, apportions the funds to the various agencies of government and issues guidelines to agencies on the permissible rate of fund expenditure during the quarters of the federal fiscal year. The comptrollers of the agencies proceed to allot the funds to the various departments within their respective agencies.

As a procurement request is initiated by a government program manager, a commitment is made which sets aside and reserves funds for the particular procurement request. When a binding document is issued, such as a purchase order, contract, grant, or cooperative agreement, the committed funds are obligated. As obligated funds are paid by government to the contractor, in discharge of contractual liability, the payment is considered an expenditure.

Regulations

In the early days of our history, Congress often passed legislation that contained both the broad policies and the specific conditions under which the purpose of the law was to be accomplished. But as Congress encountered more complex social and technical issues, it limited legislation to the broader areas and delegated authority to the executive and independent agencies to issue specific regulations to carry out the laws. In this respect, regulations may be considered delegated legislation.

The relationship of the laws of Congress to the regulations that flow from these laws may be illustrated by the *United States Code* and the *Code of Federal Regulations*. The *United States Code*, containing the current laws passed by Congress, occupies only about one third of the shelving space required for the approximately 140 volumes of the *Code of Federal Regulations*, which contain the agency regulations implementing Congressional legislation.

Regulations may be described as statements of policy or procedure, published in the *Federal Register* in accordance with prescribed rules of public notice. Regulations implement legislation, have the full force and effect of law, and can only be changed through formal rule making procedures.

Federal Register Act and Administrative Procedures Act. Prior to the passage of the Federal Register Act in 1935, there was no central processing system for the publication of regulations. Each agency had its own procedure. The public had to search out regulations on a trial and error basis which was very time consuming. Congress recognized the problem and passed the Federal Register Act to provide for the daily publication of proposed regulations, agency meetings, and final actions of all federal agencies.

As a result of the Administrative Procedures Act of 1946, the public was given an opportunity to comment on agency proposals, published in the *Federal Register*, prior to the issuance of final regulations. This review and comment process at times prevents unworkable proposals from becoming final regulations. It is incumbent on the continuing education administrator to review agency proposals that may have organizational impact either in programmatic or management areas, to contact and express points of view to any national associations with which the organization may be affiliated, and to comment to the agency directly. Keep in mind that by the time proposed rule making is published in the *Federal Register*, national associations may already have commented on the possible effects of the proposed rule making upon their members. Should your organization belong to such associations, be on the association's mailing lists, and make your views known at the earliest possible date, preferably from the highest administrative level.

Federal Register Process. Each agency must publish its regulations for each program in the *Federal Register* as follows:

1. Proposed regulations are published with requests for public comment within a specified time period—usually 30, 45, or 60 days. An agency contact person is listed with both address and telephone number, should there be any questions from the public.

2. The agency then considers the public comments and then publishes the final regulations in the *Federal Register*. The most serious comments are usully paraphrased and answered in this final rule making procedure. Should a comment or suggestion be rejected by the agency, a justification is usually provided.

3. The final regulations are sent to Congress and become effective 45 days after transmittal, unless Congress finds that the regulations are inconsistent with authorizing legislation. Should the administrator feel strongly that the agency review and analysis of his or her comments are not satisfactory or that the agency has exceeded its scope of authority in terms of the authorizing program legislation, the administrator can go directly to representatives of appropriate Congressional bodies and make a final case before the regulations become effective. This approach may be effective when done with other persons and groups who share the same concerns. A recent example is the resolution, agreed to by both the House and Senate, disapproving the Department of Education's regulations for the Law-Related Education Program authorized by the Education Amendments of 1978.

More detailed information about the *Federal Register* process is available in a booklet titled *The Federal Register: What It Is and How To Use It* (1980).

Other Statutes and Rules. In addition to program regulations, there are also cross-cutting statutes and executive branch rules. Occasionally passed by Congress to be applicable to programs on a government-wide basis, cross-cutting statutes include Title VI of the Civil Rights Act of 1964, the Intergovernmental Cooperation Act of 1968, the Joint Funding Simplification Act of 1974, and the Federal Grant and Cooperative Agreement Act of 1977. Executive Branch rules are issued primarily by the Office of Management and Budget (OMB) for government-wide application in an attempt to standardize the multitude of grant administrative requirements. These include OMB circulars such as A-95, A-102, A-110, and a host of others.

Laws and Regulations Affecting Contracts and Grants

With contracts, the government essentially procures goods or services for its own direct benefit to fulfill a specific requirement. There are no legislative matching fund requirements as with grants, but occasionally a cost-sharing contract may be required. As a result of the two leading procedural statutes relating to procurement, namely the Armed Services Procurement Act of 1947, and the Federal Property and Administrative Services Act of 1949, the entire procurement process from proposal initiation to contract termination is very well defined as compared to the grant process. The Federal Procurement Regulations (FPR) are applicable to civilian agencies and the Armed Services Procurement Regulations (ASPR), renamed and now known as the Defense Acquisition Regulations (DAR), are applicable to the military departments. For our purposes, the two regulations are essentially similar, and nearly all the civilian agencies and military departments have issued their own regulations which implement the FPR and DAR.

In recent years Congress has been attempting to create the Federal Acquisition Regulations (FAR) which would apply to all federal contracting, both military and civilian, and bring greater economy and efficiency to the contracting process. The Office of Federal Procurement Policy (OFPP), established in 1975 within OMB, is currently preparing the FAR for publication. The administrator should follow this development and obtain a copy of the FAR when issued.

Until that time, the administrator may wish to have access to the *Code of Federal Regulations.* Chapters 1 and 2 of Title 41 contain the *Federal Procurement Regulations System (Code of Federal Regulations,* 1980).

Procurement and Contracting Methods. Under the Federal Procurement Regulations, there are two methods of procurement: formal advertising and negotiation. Under either method, all contracts must be made on a competitive basis to the maximum practicable extent.

Formal advertising means procurement (typically over $10,000) by the government through competitive bids and awards utilizing the following basic steps:

1. Preparation of an *Invitation for Bids* (IFB), describing the requirements of the government clearly, accurately, and completely.

2. Publicizing the IFB through distribution to prospective bidders in sufficient time to enable such bidders to prepare and submit bids by the closing time for receipt of bids, usually 20 to 30 days after issuance of the IFB. Publicity may be through mailing lists, newspaper advertising, or the *Commerce Business Daily.*

3. Submission of sealed bids by prospective contractors.

4. Awarding the contract after sealed bids are publicly opened, to the lowest responsible and responsive bidder.

Contracts awarded after formal advertising are of the firm fixed price type in which the contractor is paid a stated amount of money for delivery of the product or service without regard to the actual cost to the contractor. If the contractor has good cost control, profit margins may be widened. By the same token, should there be a cost overrun, the contractor has to absorb the additional costs and the resulting financial loss.

To be considered for award, the bid must be responsive in all material respects to the IFB. This means that the bid must be properly completed, signed by an authorized official of the prospective contracting agency, and submitted to the government precisely in accordance with the

IFB instructions. Should there be any deviations, the bid may be considered nonresponsive to the solicitation and not considered for award. Please note that this "formal" competitive procedure is designed to afford all potential contractors the same opportunity to do business with the government. All are treated equally, must bid to the same specifications, and must accept the same conditions. The government consistently maintains the integrity of this process, even if it has to pay more money for the goods and services procured.

A prospective contractor must also be responsible and meet the following requirements:

1. Have adequate financial resources.

2. Be able to comply with the required or proposed delivery or performance schedule.

3. Have a satisfactory record of performance. Unsatisfactory past performance ordinarily classifies a contractor as irresponsible.

4. Have a satisfactory record of integrity and business ethics.

5. Have the necessary organization, experience, operational controls, and technical skills to perform the work.

Negotiation, on the other hand, does not involve a rigid set of formal procedures and generally means a procurement through a series of offers and counteroffers until a satisfactory agreement is reached by the contracting parties. It is characterized by the issuance of a request for proposals (RFP), similar to an IFB, in response to which proposals are received and evaluated. The government then negotiates with prospective contractors found to be within a competitive range, requests best and final offers, and awards the contract. Such procurement must be on a competitive basis to the maximum practical extent and must fit within one of fifteen categories which the contracting officer or a higher authority must certify in advance of negotiation. Some categories particularly useful to nonprofit agencies include (1) purchases not in excess of $10,000, (2) services of educational institutions, (3) situations where it is impractical to secure competition (commonly called a *sole source procurement*), and (4) experimental, development, or research work (*Government Contract Principles*, 1980, pp. 5–9).

Contracts awarded after negotiation may be either firm fixed price, as previously described, or the cost reimbursement type which provides for payment of allowable costs incurred in contract performance up to the amount prescribed in the contract. This type of contract establishes an estimate of total cost for the purpose of obligation of funds and a ceiling which the contractors may not exceed (except at their own risk) without prior approval and subsequent ratification by the government's contracting officer. The various cost contracts are: (1) cost reimbursement only, (2) cost sharing, (3) cost plus incentive fee, (4) cost plus fixed fee, and (5) cost plus award fee. For further information on government procurement see *Government Contract Principles* (1980).

Grants. With grants, there is no regulatory equivalent to the FPR and DAR. Rather, Cappalli's recent research includes examination not only of sixty-six separate grant statutes ranging from a few to several hundred pages in length but also of approximately four hundred grant program regulations (Cappalli, 1979). Noted before, Congress has enacted some government-wide "cross-cutting" statutes and OMB has attempted to standardize the various grant requirements through the issuance of its circular directives for government-wide application.

Federal Grant and Cooperative Agreement Act of 1977 (Public Law 95-224). Congress found that there was a need to distinguish assistance relationships from procurement relationships and thereby standardize usage and clarify the meaning of the legal instruments which reflect such relationships. Under the Act, each executive agency is authorized and directed to enter into and use types of contracts, grant agreements, or cooperative agreements as appropriate to the circumstances.

Procurement contracts are to be used as the legal instrument reflecting a relationship between the federal government and a state or local government or other recipient whenever the principal purpose is the acquisition, by purchase, lease, or barter, of property or services for the direct benefit or use of the federal government.

Grant agreements are to be used whenever the principal purpose of the relationship is the transfer of money, property, services, or anything of value to a state or local government or other recipient in order to accomplish a public purpose of support or stimulation authorized by federal statute and where no substantial involvement is anticipated between the executive agency and the grantee during performance of the contemplated activity.

Cooperative agreements are to be used whenever the principal purpose of the relationship is the same as in grants agreements above and where substantial involvement is anticipated between the executive agency and the recipient during performance of the contemplated activity.

One other item in the Act is worthy of note. The authority to make contracts, grants, and cooperative agreements for the conduct of basic or applied scientific research at nonprofit institutions of higher education or at nonprofit organizations, whose primary purpose is the conduct of scientific research, includes discretionary authority to vest in such institutions or organizations title to equipment or other tangible personal property purchased with such funds.

OMB Circular A-95. The A-95 review process is a procedure for coordinating federal and federally assisted grant programs and projects with each other and with state, regional, and local plans and programs. The circular has four major sections, but the most important is the project notification and review system which provides an opportunity for state and local governments to review, through their established clearinghouses, applications for federal grants under approximately 250 different programs. Generally, these grant programs are not research programs, but rather social or public works programs which require some type of state or local coordination.

The applicant files a notice of intent to apply under the federal program to the state and areawide A-95 clearinghouses in the jurisdiction in which the proposed project is to be located. The applicant provides appropriate information and asks if the clearinghouses are interested in reviewing the application. The clearinghouses either (1) ignore the notice, in which case the applicant waits the required thirty days and proceeds with the application; (2) write back indicating that they do not yet have any opinions about the proposed project, but would like to review it after it is in final form; or (3) write back stating that they have some ideas (that is, they think it may be unnecessary, duplicative, or inconsistent with state and local plans) and think a coordinated approach is needed with other interested groups. If this is the type of advice given, an applicant is obligated to follow up and take appropriate action.

If the clearinghouses wish to see the final application, it must be sent to them for comments which must also be included with the application to the federal agency which, in turn, reviews such comments as a part of its funding evaluation.

One other point must be noted. If an application must be made jointly with another organization, any differences between the organizations must be resolved before either one applies to the federal grant program. If the differences cannot be resolved, a statement must be included indicating what steps were taken to resolve differences and the status at the time of submission.

Grant Administrative Circulars. OMB Circular A-102, "Uniform Administrative Requirements for Grants-in-Aid to State and Local Governments" and OMB Circular A-110, "Grants and Agreements with Institutions of Higher Education, Hospitals and Other Nonprofit Organizations" provide uniform methods for grant administration. By standardizing administrative procedures on a government-wide basis, the OMB circulars make it easier for the grantee to deal with more than one federal agency because all federal agencies are required to be consistent with the circular requirements. Agencies are prohibited from altering, modifying, or going beyond such requirements unless OMB gives prior authorization. Some of the subjects included in these circulars are: (1) records retention, (2) grant-related income, (3) cost sharing and matching, (4) financial reporting requirements, (5) suspension and termination procedures, and numerous others—all of which are important to effective programmatic, financial, and legal administration of projects.

Assurances. With every grant application, the prospective grantee's authorized representative usually must assure the government that it will comply with various statutes. With contracts, such assurances are known as *representations and certifications* which also require signature by the contractor's authorized representative. Examples are:

1. Title VI of the Civil Rights Act of 1964 which prohibits discrimination on the basis of race, color or national origin.

2. Title IX of the Education Amendments of 1972 which prohibits discrimination on the basis of sex.

3. Section 504 of the Rehabilitation Act of 1973 which prohibits discrimination on the basis of handicap.

4. The Age Discrimination Act of 1975 which prohibits discrimination on the basis of age.

5. Human Subjects Review (45 CFR 46) which requires the contractor to safeguard the rights and welfare of human subjects who may be placed "at risk" because of their participation in a project. An individual is at risk if he or she may be exposed to the possibility of physical, psychological, or social injury.

6. Laboratory Animal Welfare Act of 1966 which provides for the care, handling, and treatment of warm-blooded animals used for research or teaching. While the organization may sign these and other required assurances, remember that such assurances are subject to cognizant agency review and audit.

Cost Principles: Direct and Indirect Costs. The administrator must be aware of the mandatory federal cost principles applicable to the organization. When *either* a federal contract or grant is received, the organization must account for all project costs under the appropriate set of cost principles: (1) commercial organizations, Federal Procurement Regulations (FPR) Subpart 1-15.2; (2) state and local governments, OMB Circular A-87; (3) institutions of higher education, OMB Circular A-21; and (4) other nonprofit organizations, OMB Circular A-122.

The total cost of a contract or grant is the sum of direct and indirect costs allocable to the project during its effective period. A direct cost is any cost which can be identified specifically with a particular research project or instructional activity, or which can be directly assigned to such activities relatively easily and with a high degree of accuracy. An indirect cost is one that has been incurred for common or joint objectives and, therefore, cannot be identified specifically with a particular research project or instructional activity. To avoid audit disallowance, both direct and indirect costs must be allowable under the applicable cost principles, reasonable, and allocable to the project.

Indirect cost rates are usually expressed as a percentage of total direct labor or total direct costs. The following example shows, in principle, how an indirect cost rate might be developed for a commercial organization. During the organization's fiscal year, the following indirect expenses were incurred for general and administrative support:

President's salary and fringe benefits	$50,000	
Office rental (on short-term lease)	8,000	Allowable under FPR 1-15.2
Telephone	2,000	
Interest expense	10,000	
Contribution to XYZ University	1,000	Not allowable under FPR 1-15.2
Entertainment costs	2,000	
Total	$73,000	

The organization's total direct labor expended on projects was $500,000. What is the indirect cost rate? Under the federal cost principles for commercial organizations (FPR 1-15.2), only the president's salary and fringe benefits, office rental, and telephone would be allowable indirect expenses. The other costs are specifically not allowable under the federal cost principles as direct or indirect expenses. Therefore, the indirect cost rate for this organizational component would be $60,000 divided by $500,000 or 12 percent of total direct costs. This method of indirect cost collection should be more beneficial to the organization than the other method of calculation, namely the total direct cost approach. As labor is paid in an organization, indirect cost is immediately incurred and billable to the government. If, however, the total direct cost method is used, the organization must wait on supplier's invoices and pay them before billing for indirect cost. Through utilization of a direct labor rate, organizational cash flow should be enhanced.

If an organization does not have an audited indirect cost rate and wishes to establish one, its first step would be to acquire the federal cost principles document appropriate to its type of organization, as identified above. Using the established principles, the organization's comptroller conducts an indirect cost study and submits it to the appropriate cognizant audit agency for review. The audit agency will then negotiate an indirect cost rate with the organization, which results in a negotiated agreement. Such an agreement may contain several different rates, including, for example, on- and off-site instruction, and on- and off-site research rates. The cognizant audit agency for most nonprofit organizations is normally the appropriate regional audit agency of the U.S. Department of Health and Human Services. A recently published pamphlet, "Direct and Indirect Costs of Research at Colleges and Universities," is a helpful exposition of this complex topic (1981).

Legal Considerations. Both contracts and grants are accompanied by a whole host of terms and conditions or general provisions with which the contractor or grantee must comply. While a grant may be more flexible and less specific in its approach than a contract, both are contractual and legally enforceable instruments. As such, the administrator should read each contract or grant document and understand what it says. If there are questions or if provisions are "incorporated by reference" and not included with the contract or grant package, telephone the agency and have the provisions sent to you. Also, make certain to review the scope of work. Is it what your organization promised? There must be clear understandings at the outset.

To relate a recent personal experience, a federal agency sent a grant agreement to the American University with specification that, through acceptance of the grant, university employees would be required to abide by the Federal Hatch Act which would limit their political activity. Of course, in an academic institution, such an idea is absurd at best. After two months of negotiation with the agency and with assistance from a national association, the condition was finally deleted. *Read the contract or grant very carefully indeed—and negotiate!*

Audit. The auditor performs (1) financial/compliance audits, (2) economy/efficiency audits, and (3) program performance or results audits. Should an auditor telephone for an appointment, the administrator should first confirm that the auditor is from an appropriate audit agency and that the audit request covers contracts or grants that are still auditable. Often, the time period during which the government has the right to audit has passed. If all is in order, work closely with your organization's business or sponsored programs office to collect the necessary information and data, arrange for personnel to be available, and provide appropriate facilities for the auditor.

Summary

There is a plethora of laws and regulations that govern who may apply for contracts and grants, how awards are to be made, how projects are to be managed and administered, and what happens after the project is completed. Continuing education project administrators who want to be successful will need to become sufficiently familiar with the requirements of their projects in order to avoid difficulties and use the total system to their advantage.

References

Cappalli, R. B. *Rights and Remedies under Federal Grants.* Washington, D.C.: The Bureau of National Affairs, 1979.

Code of Federal Regulations. Title 41: Public Contracts and Property Management. Washington, D.C.: Government Printing Office, July 1, 1980.

"Cost Principles for Educational Institutions." (OMB Circular No. A-21). *Federal Register,* March 6, 1979, *44* (45). Washington, D.C.: U.S. Office of Management and Budget, 1979.

"Cost Principles for Nonprofit Organizations." (OMB Circular No. A-122). *Federal Register*, July 8, 1980, *45* (132). Washington, D.C.: U.S. Office of Management and Budget, 1980.

"Cost Principles for State and Local Governments." (OMB Circular No. A-87). *Federal Register*, January 28, 1981, *46* (18). Washington, D.C.: U.S. Office of Management and Budget, 1981. (Replaces FMC 74-4)

"Direct and Indirect Costs of Research at Colleges and Universities." Washington, D.C.: American Council on Education and Council of Governmental Relations, National Association of College and University Business Officers, 1981.

"Evaluation, Review, and Coordination of Federal and Federally-Assisted Programs and Projects." (OMB Circular No. A-95). *Federal Register*, January 13, 1976, *41* (8). Washington, D.C.: U.S. Office of Management and Budget, 1976.

The Federal Register: What It Is and How to Use It. Washington, D.C.: Office of the Federal Register, 1980.

Office of the General Counsel, U.S. General Accounting Office. *Government Contract Principles*. Washington, D.C.: Government Printing Office, 1980.

"Uniform Administrative Requirements for Grants and Agreements with Institutions of Higher Education, Hospitals, and Other Non-Profit Organizations." (OMB Circular No. A-110). *Federal Register*, July 30, 1976, *41* (148). Washington, D.C.: U.S. Office of Management and Budget, 1976.

"Uniform Administrative Requirements for Grants-in-Aid to State and Local Governments." (OMB Circular No. A-102). *Federal Register*, September 12, 1977, *42* (176). Washington, D.C.: U.S. Office of Management and Budget, 1977.

U.S. Department of Defense. *Manual for Contract Pricing*. Chicago, Ill.: Commerce Clearing House, 1975.

Stanley M. Matelski is director of program development and contract/grant administration at the American University, Washington, D.C. Formerly he was assistant director of the office of sponsored programs, University of Maryland at College Park.

Cost recovery from fees has been used as a reason for not seeking private support, but is a strong reason for doing so.

Fund Raising for Continuing Education

Maurice Atkinson

Rapidly declining federal support calls for new and increasing attention to private sector funding possibilities for continuing education. Those who serve community agencies, YMCAs, YWCAs, hospitals, and museums already know the importance of this from long-time pursuit of private funds. College, university, public school adult education, and community education administrators are beginning to realize it.

"Continuing education is the last of the activities of universities to take an interest in outside funding. Instruction has sought alumni support and endowed chairs. Research has set up foundations to receive external support. But in continuing education, we not only receive little outside support, we are asked to be largely self-supporting through fees charged the attending students" (1979). These remarks of William L. Turner, Vice Chancellor for Extension and Public Service at North Carolina State University, underscore continuing education's need for private sector support.

While the funding needs of continuing education are exacerbated by sweeping cuts in federal and state budgets for education, presidents and development officers are beginning to focus their attention on the importance of private funding for continuing education, not only because of its needs, but also because continuing education has a broad constituency of

J. Buskey (Ed.). *New Directions for Continuing Education: Attracting External Funds for Continuing Education,* no. 12. San Francisco: Jossey-Bass, December 1981.

potential individual and corporate donors enrolled in its programs. When properly coordinated, continuing education can aid in the total funding of the parent organization as well as of itself.

Demographics of aging population, higher average age of student bodies, lower elementary school enrollment, and the leveling of higher education enrollment mean that education is becoming a lifelong learning process and must be so marketed.

No one has stated the philosophy of continuing education as a lifelong learning process so well or been more generous to it than the W. K. Kellogg Foundation. In an interview, Arlon E. Elser, former vice chancellor at the University of Pittsburgh, now program director for education at the Kellogg Foundation, declared: "The principal development in continuing education is that college and university administrators are awakening to its value. They see it as their way to survive."

Differences Between Government Grants and Private Funding

With cuts in federal funding, its probable selective continuance, and the greater need for private funding, it is well to note the similarities and differences between government grants and private funding.

Similarities. Both federal grants and substantial private gifts require written proposals. In neither case will verbal solicitation alone work. Conversation might result in a four-figure private gift, but it will not produce a five-, six-, or seven-figure gift. Federal grants require very rigid guidelines and deadlines, and so do certain private foundation applications. Federal grants are the result of tax money appropriations. Private gifts result from the humane concern of private parties, often using tax-saving incentives authorized by Congress or state legislatures. Both types of proposals require skill and the ability to deal with deadlines and be persuasive with a variety of individuals. Federal government proposals, however, relate to a given program; successful private funding proposals often incorporate a variety of programs to give the private donor a choice. The federal grantseeker and the private fund raiser have full-time jobs.

Differences. The organization must decide whether full funding, partial support, or isolated programs can be funded best by public or private sources. Because both markets seem to require concentration, the basic decision is whether to employ a grantseeker or a fund raiser—synonymous terms but separated in practice. The latter has a broader choice because there are still more individual, corporate, and foundation prospects than government agencies. Freed from ironclad forms and reporting procedures, the fund raiser nevertheless should recognize that voluntary reporting to the private donor on the use of funds is as important as required reporting to the government agency.

Volunteers. In the use of the volunteer, private fund raising departs widely from government grantsmanship. Few volunteers are used in seeking and soliciting federal grants. Conversely, their use in private fund raising is indispensable, in such ways as donating exemplary gifts, evaluating prospects, soliciting peers, enlisting other workers, and in increasing the number of members of committees and divisions of annual or capital campaigns. Volunteers who are carefully cultivated and selected from among current participants in continuing education programs or from among executives of corporations whose employees benefit from programs, can create a "web" of influence which helps secure private gifts. For example, A is chief executive officer of a corporation whose middle management personnel are enrolled in time study programs, thus providing a direct reason why A might contribute, serve on your campaign committee, or both. However, A has a brother-in-law, B, who is on the board of directors of another corporation, which is a likely prospect for additional support. Moreover, B has a spouse (A's sister) who is president of an organization seeking expansion of reading courses for minority groups, which the continuing education center will offer next spring. Furthermore, A and B have a friend C, who needs a charitable tax deduction on a large end-of-the-year profit. Identifying and knowing those who attend and benefit by programs is the first step toward securing greater private funding.

Organizing Volunteers

Identification. Obviously, the process of identifying volunteers needs to go beyond mere class enrollment forms. If the form provides for job title, it could be helpful. "Affluent" addresses are useful indicators of ability to give. Questionnaires may be circulated. The instructor's knowledge of individuals enrolled in his or her classes is paramount. All this information should be incorporated on cards, lists, or printouts.

A man enrolled in a night Spanish course may be a wealthy widower with no heirs. A woman learning to operate a microwave oven in an agricultural extension course may live in the wealthiest part of town. A guest lecturer on gourmet cooking may know wealthy restaurateurs.

During a dry legislator's attack on a wine-tasting course at a southeastern university, a student in the course came to its defense. Only then did the dean of continuing education learn the student was a millionaire and a powerful man in the state.

Advisory Councils and Support Groups. From the identification process, known outside supporters of continuing education, corporate leaders, and potential donors, administrators can then form program advisory councils. It is better for the administrator to enlist a few, and then ask them to invite others. Once the council has been formed, it cannot be put "on hold" or interest will fade. Regular meetings of the advisory council(s) must be held to inform members of the program activities of the continuing education agency; their advice on the content of future programs should be sought. Only after such cultivation can you call upon these leaders to organize and participate in a fund-raising campaign. Meanwhile staff solicitation of funds can be underway, so that the support group will be encouraged by some success.

Institutional Recognition of Funding Needs

Strategy. With the organization of the advisory council or other support group, the continuing education administrator is in a stronger position to convince the central administration, development office, or foundation to recognize the department's fund-raising needs and potential. Budgeting for a departmental fund raiser previously described should be sought, or else someone from the central development office should be assigned to oversee the effort.

It is a mistake for continuing education, or any other department to engage in isolated and conflicting solicitation. The people who will resent this most are the prospective donors. No matter how generous, prospects take a dim view of an institution whose school of engineering calls on them one week, school of continuing education the next, followed by an all-university campaign call a few weeks later!

In presenting its rationale for funding help from central administration, continuing education has a strong case:

1. Ironically, the excuse given in the past for not seeking private support for continuing education is the strongest possible rationale for such support: the ratio of earned income to expense provided by the fees charged. Private donors often regard earned income of nonprofit organizations in the same high degree as profits to private enterprise. Income from fees, in relative degrees, shows the department is sound and worthy of support.

2. In pursuing corporate gifts, the organization's development department constantly seeks to identify service relationships with hundreds of companies. The continuing education programs often represent the major, and sometimes the only, linkage with potential corporate donors. In a recent capital campaign, for example, we found the only linkage with an international corporation was a university continuing education closed circuit classroom program for engineers in company plants.

A college on the Atlantic Coast had been unable to cultivate top corporate officers—even get them on the telephone—until that college's continuing education department offered seminars leading to MBA degrees for vice presidents. A major local manufacturer underwrote costs. In a subsequent capital campaign, two of the companies enrolled made substantial five-figure gifts, while the chief executive officer of one company became a member of the college's board of trustees. In another instance, a major department store chain gave $60,000 to a southern school to sponsor fellowships for women executives whose careers had been interrupted.

Continuing education programs in rural areas frequently involve relationships with major landholders. Gifts of land for resale by institutions probably are the major form of individual giving to institutions that serve agriculture. In 1980, individuals gave 83.7 percent of total contributions to American philanthropy, according to *Giving USA* (1981, p. 7). Undoubtedly, many of those gifts involved real estate holdings.

These should be telling arguments in obtaining staff support for private fund-raising. With staffing and support groups in place, the continuing education unit can make further plans to campaign for private support. These plans involve understanding the differences between annual and capital campaigns and their interrelationships with institutions and donors.

Annual Campaigns

It is safe to say that continuing education should not undertake major capital campaigns until it has secured a solid base of annual funding from a number of donors. The exception would be capital programs, such as construction of a conference center or faculty development which are part of a total campus campaign.

Annual giving represents a yearly effort by an organization to raise a specific sum generally to fill the gaps between budget allocation, earned income, and expense. The amount of annual funds sought increases each year, due to inflation, loss of government support, and/or lack of endowment. Annual campaigns generally seek recurring but increased three- to four-figure gifts from a broad base of donors, alumni, and friends. Therefore, it involves the organization of many workers into teams, not unlike those used in United Fund campaigns. For mop-up operations, it may involve direct mail or telephone contact. Staff support is critical. In addition, the support groups previously mentioned can provide the organizational nucleus for annual programs.

After annual giving funds have been established, an alternative is to incorporate the annual needs of the continuing education unit into the capital campaign of the larger organization or institution. This is done for three reasons: (1) to give annual donors an opportunity to make additional one-time gifts to the capital campaign, (2) to ensure that higher levels of annual giving are maintained during the capital drive, and (3) for ease in computer accounting.

Capital Campaigns

Capital campaigns seek funds for specified purposes in a well-documented list of needs: construction, faculty development, scholarships, equipment, and endowment. A capital campaign, unlike annual giving, is nonrecurring in the sense that it should be undertaken infrequently over a period of years. Therefore, it does not relate to annual deficits or loss of support. An erroneous concept is that a capital campaign includes only "brick and mortar," although it frequently does. In continuing education, it might include the construction of a new conference center or the conversion of a hotel into a conference center. More accurately, a capital campaign simply means gifts from donor assets, usually over a pledge period of three to five tax years, instead of from the donor's current income. If the donor's income is substantial, however, and vulnerable to high taxes, the donor may elect to make a pledge from current income. Again, the strategy of incorporating continuing education's capital needs into the total institutional package should be explored.

Pledges and Tax Advantages of Giving

In general, making a gift in installments, or *pledging*, permits a donor to make a much larger contribution than with a one-time gift. For example, a donor may make a pledge to be fulfilled in a 36-month period (three calendar years), and by timing the payments, extend those payments over four tax years. In practice, the donor would contribute one fourth of the gift at the time the pledge was made and similar amounts in the next three succeeding anniversary months.

While most donors give out of goodwill or deep emotional commitment to the causes they believe in, tax incentives are of enormous advantage in soliciting gifts. Federal income and estate tax laws, as well as state tax statutes, provide substantial deductions for charitable givers. In the case of married couples with $20,000 of taxable income, the cost of a $1,000 contribution may be only $760. If a couple has $215,000 of taxable income, the cost per $1,000 is less than one third of that amount. Under the Economic Recovery Tax Act of 1981, a corporation giving up to 10 percent or less of its net income per tax year may deduct 46 percent of its charitable contributions. The local office of the Internal Revenue Service can provide an excellent booklet on charitable tax deductions.

Case Statement

Before going out to seek pledges in an annual or capital campaign, put your case in writing, not only because you will need it as a guide for campaign literature, but also because it will alert your organization to your strengths and weaknesses. Continuing education can make a strong case for the following: number of people served, economic impact on the community, the lifelong learning process, programs for the disadvantaged, service to industry, and many others.

Laws of Campaigning

Because of continuing education's broad constituency and its newness to private fund raising, here are some rules experience has shown will work well for staff and volunteer fund raisers:

1. Research the prospect. Successful fund raising is "90 percent research and 10 percent solicitations." How do prospect and family relate to your program? What are their interests? What's in it for them?

2. Seek pledges.

3. Go after the big gifts first. Another 90-10 rule is that "10 percent of the people give 90 percent of the money."

4. Be quiet about it. Get big gifts in before announcing a campaign. Announcing a campaign with an empty till invites failure, but substantial gifts challenge others to give. Announce gifts in the order of size. Announcing a small gift invites more capable donors to do the same. The time to announce a campaign, or any gifts thereto, is after substantial gifts are in hand.

5. Don't compete with other elements of your organization in calling on the same prospects. Don't let them compete with you.

6. Make written proposals for specific amounts. Past experience with government proposals will stand the continuing education fund raiser in good stead and confine the solicitation to what is needed rather than to chance, particularly where several people may be involved in making the decision to donate funds.

Summary

In the face of federal and state cuts, inflation, and shifts in education clientele, the quest for private funds will become even more important in the years ahead. Because of its link to millions of potentially generous donors, continuing education—to mix a metaphor—can sit in the cat-bird seat of private funding instead of hiding its light under a bushel.

References

Giving USA. Annual Report for 1980. New York: American Association of Fund-Raising Counsel, 1981.

Turner, W. L. "Remarks." Delivered to the Council on Extension and Continuing Education, National Association of State Universities and Land Grant Colleges, Washington, D.C., November 1979.

Maurice Atkinson is vice president of operations,
John Grenzebach and Associates, Inc., Chicago, Illinois.
He and his firm are fund raising consultants to colleges,
universities, hospitals, YMCAs, YWCAs, community
centers, and arts organizations.

*Suit the action to the word, the word to
the action—Shakespeare.*

Glossary of Terms Relating to External Funding

John H. Buskey

The world of grantsmanship and fund raising has its own special language, technical terms, and jargon. This glossary has been compiled over several years from many sources as an aid to persons seeking external funding for their agencies.

Major contributions to the glossary have been made by Jessie Ulin, formerly project director of the Region III Adult Education Staff Development Project at the University of Maryland University College, and Carl Mueller, grants and contracts fiscal manager, University of Nebraska-Lincoln. Authors of chapters in this sourcebook have reviewed the glossary and several have recommended additions, deletions, and modifications.

Appropriation. A federal, state, or local legislative enactment which allows government agencies to incur obligations to spend or lend money during specified time periods, usually a fiscal year. The funds appropriated for a fiscal year are sometimes more than the obligations or outlays within that year due to the long-range nature of some programs (particularly construction projects). Congress may appropriate funds only on the basis of an existing authorization. (See *Authorization.*)

Authorization. Basic substantive legislation which sets up a program or agency. Such legislation sometimes sets limits on the amount that can subsequently be appropriated but does not actually provide money or

J. Buskey (Ed.). *New Directions for Continuing Education: Attracting External Funds for Continuing Education,* no. 12. San Francisco: Jossey-Bass, December 1981.

guarantee that monies will be appropriated in any given fiscal year. (See *Appropriation.*)

Award. The document, which may be a letter, a special form, or a contract document, prescribing the amount of funds and restrictions imposed on an agreement between two parties. The federal government commonly uses three basic types of award instruments. (See *Contract, Cooperative Agreements,* and *Grant.*)

Budget. The estimated cost of performance of the project as set forth in a proposal or in the notification of grant award or contract.

Contract. A legal instrument reflecting a relationship between two parties, such as between a federal government agency and a state or local government or other recipient whenever the principal purpose of the instrument is the acquisition by purchase, lease, or barter, of property or services for the direct benefit or use of the federal government. (See *Contract types, Cooperative agreements,* and *Grant.*)

Contract types. There are many types of contracts, but they are essentially variations of either the firm-fixed-price (lump sum) contract awarded as a result of a formally advertised invitation for bids (IFB), or the cost reimbursement contract, which is awarded as the result of a request for proposal (RFP). Variations include fixed-price with escalation, fixed-price incentive, cost-plus-incentive, cost-plus-a-fixed-fee, time and materials, and others.

Cooperative agreements. An award instrument that is used when it is anticipated that the proposed project may require substantial involvement of the federal agency in controlling the activities of the project or in executing the project. It is considered to be an "assistance relationship," and therefore more similar to a grant than to a contract. This category of award was created by the Federal Grant and Cooperative Agreement Act of 1977, P. L. 95–224.

Cost sharing. (See *Matching contributions.*)

Direct costs. Expenses which can be itemized and for which vouchers or payroll records can be presented for payment. They include salaries and wages, fringe benefits, supplies, travel, communication, equipment, computers, rentals, printing, duplication and so forth.

Documentation. The "paper trail" that any project generates in keeping track of its staff, clients, services, and budget. Documentation is the raw material used to evaluate the success of a project.

Employee benefits (fringe benefits). Direct expenditures by an organization on behalf of its employees for such items as workmen's compensation, disability insurance, unemployment compensation, Social Security, life and health insurance, retirement, and graduate student tuition remission. Usually fringe benefits are calculated as a percentage of salaries.

Encumbrance. A purchase order for goods or services which has been issued but not paid.

Estimated income. The maximum amount of grant or contract funds to be received by the institution, assuming the full amount of the award is expended.

Evaluation. The appraisal seeking to measure the extent to which an activity or program has or has not attained the established objectives.

Evaluation, external. Sometimes defined as *third-party evaluations,* the external evaluation is conducted by individuals who are not directly involved in the process, procedure, or program being assessed.

Evaluation, formative (process evaluation). The first phase of a two-phase evaluation strategy, this phase examines the project while it is ongoing and functioning. Data from this phase can be used to make adjustments in the daily operation of the project. (See *Evaluation, summative.*)

Evaluation, internal. Use of regular project staff for assessing the extent to which the project is achieving its objectives.

Evaluation, summative. The second phase of a two-part evaluation strategy, this phase examines the outcomes or products of what the project produced. It is done at the end of the project time period. (See *Evaluation, formative.*)

Expenditure. A payment of cash for goods or services.

Expenditure account. The account to which grant or contract expenses are charged.

Fiscal year (FY). Usually a 12-month period for which funds are appropriated and during which expenditures must be made. The federal fiscal year runs from October 1 to September 30 and is designated by the calendar year in which it ends. For example, FY 1982 covers the period October 1,1981 to September 30, 1982. Most state and local governments have July 1 to June 30 fiscal years. The fiscal year of many corporations is the same as the calendar year, January 1 to December 31.

Grant. A legal instrument reflecting a relationship between a federal government agency and a state or local government or other recipient whenever the principal purpose of the relationship is the transfer of money, property, services or anything of value to the recipient to accomplish a public purpose of support or stimulation. In the private sector, a grant is a formal gift of money, property, services, or anything of value for designated or unrestricted purposes. (See *Contract* and *Cooperative agreements.*)

Grant or contract officer. The funding agency employee who is authorized to execute an award document and is responsible for the financial and legal administration of the grant or contract on behalf of the funding organization. He or she is the only person authorized to approve amendments to the award. (See *Program officer.*)

Grant or contract period (project period). The period of time specified in the grant or contract award during which costs may be charged against the project.

Grantee (contractor). The agency, institution, or organization named in the grant or contract as the recipient.

Guidelines. A document or set of documents published by individual federal or other public or private agencies which contain application forms and information about program priorities for use by applicant organizations. The companion documents for contracts are Invitations for Bids (IFB) or Requests for Proposals (RFP). Some foundations also publish specific guidelines to assist applicants in preparing proposals.

Income account. Account in which grant or contract support dollars are deposited.

Indirect cost rate. A percentage rate, usually of salaries or total direct costs, used to compute the amount of indirect cost to be charged to a grant or contract.

Indirect costs (overhead). Costs that are incurred for common or joint objectives, but which are difficult to itemize on a project-by-project basis, such as business office services, physical plant operation, general administration, and library services. Government agencies allow contract or grant recipients to use an approved indirect cost rate to compensate for these expenditures.

Invitation for bids (IFB). The formal advertisement of a proposed government procurement requesting competitive bids. The IFB usually results in a firm-fixed-price contract.

Letter of credit. A federal payment system designed to provide the payee with its cash needs as they arise rather than a single advance payment or payment upon completion of the terms of the grant or contract.

Letter of intent. A brief letter containing a description of a proposed project, an estimated budget, and information on the applicant. Sometimes it is required to allow the funding agency to screen out ineligible applicants or projects not consistent with the program's priorities. This screening saves considerable time for both the agency and the applicant.

Matching contributions. The portion of costs relating to grant-supported activity which is borne by the recipient agency (the grantee). The required extent of matching contributions or "in-kind" support is set by the funding agency and is usually a percentage of the funds provided by the granting agency. Matching gifts may also be offered by private donors as a challenge to other donors.

Multiplier effect. To increase the original amount by multiplying the original by a factor greater than one.

Needs assessment. A survey and analysis of needs for a proposed project, which usually includes symptoms, causes, a description of the population, and related data.

Pledges. A formal commitment made by a donor for payment of a total sum in installments over a period of time.

Priorities. Funding agencies develop annual program plans which include objectives and areas of emphasis. The areas of emphasis are called priorities and the agency awards contracts or grants for projects which most closely relate to those priorities. Priorities for federal grant programs are published in the *Federal Register.*

Program officer. The funding agency's employee who is responsible for monitoring the technical content or program aspects of grants or contracts. (See *Grant or contract officer.)*

Project director (principal investigator). The person responsible for directing and managing the project of the grantee or contractor.

Proposal. A written document requesting financial support to undertake a project or provide goods or services.

Proposal, request for (RFP). A document issued by a government agency which announced a proposed negotiated procurement and which solicits competitive bids. The RFP may result in either a firm fixed price or a cost reimbursement contract.

Site visit. Funding agencies occasionally visit the actual project faciliies to look around and get a feel for the applicant's organization. The site visit may be the last step in the application process before notification of funding.

Sponsored project. A specific activity or program financed by funds other than those of the regular budget of the recipient organization. Usually such programs are financed through grant or contract awards from government agencies, private foundations, or other private sources.

Target population. The intended beneficiaries of a program or service project. Also known as client population.

Terms and conditions. Document(s) incorporated into every contract or grant which set forth the specific laws and regulations or private organization requirements which govern performance, management, and financial administration of the project. Included are numerous paragraphs of which some are special and unique to a particular project. However, most items are general and apply to all awards of a particular type.

Third user of knowledge. Application of knowledge has an arbitrarily selected point of origin which commences with the teacher. The teacher, learner, and applier represent, respectively, the first, second, and third users of knowledge.

References

Shakespeare, W. "Hamlet, Prince of Denmark," Act II, sc II, line 19. In H. Craig Ed.), *The Complete Works of Shakespeare.* Glenview, Ill.: Scott, Foresman, 1951.

128

*John H. Buskey is associate dean of continuing studies and
assistant professor of adult and continuing education at the
University of Nebraska-Lincoln. He has had nearly fifteen
years experience as a proposal writer and project director, and
regularly conducts workshops and seminars on proposal
writing and grantsmanship.*

Index

follow-up, 22, 35, 73; proposal items required by, 12-13; research on, 34-35; review process of, 8-9, 14-16; rules and regulations of, 80, 103-114; systematic search for, 32-35; trends in, 29-30; types of, 30-32. *See also* External support; Foundations; Government agencies

G

General Electric Information Services Company, 35, 36
Glass, S. A., 73, 77
Goal: defined, 42; establishment of, in proposal development, 10; in mission statement, 20
Government agencies: authorizing legislation for, 65; block grants from, 30-31; criteria of, 65-66; expectations of, 63-70; as funding sources, 30-31; future support by, 70; information sources on, 32-33; instructions by, 65; purposes of, 63; regulations for, 65, 103-114; requirements of, 65-66; review process by, 14, 65-67; self-interest of, 64-65. *See also* Local government; State government
Grant agreements, 109
Grant or contract officer, 15-16, 125
Grant or contract period, 125
Grantee, 125
Grants: block, 30-31; contracts different from, 95-96, 97; defined, 125; eligibility for, 96; fund raising compared to, 116-117; regulations on, 109; specifications for, 95-96. *See also* External support; Proposals
Greensboro, North Carolina, corporate training needs in, 10
Gross, M., 62
Guidelines, 126

H

Haas Fund, 37
Hall, M., 53, 62
Hallahan, K. M., 76, 77
Harris, J. B., 2, 89-94
Hartman, L., 71, 76, 77
Hatch Act, 113
Hegeland, H., 89, 94

Hendricks, W., 87
Higher Education Act, Title I of, 38
Hill Family Foundation, 75
Hillman, H., 32, 39, 73, 76, 77
Hirsch, E., 71n
Hotel Association of Michigan, 91
Human Subjects Review, 111

I

Income account, 126
Indirect costs: in budget, 57, 60-61; defined, 126; regulations on, 111-112
Information: card file for, 21-22; and contact follow-up, 22, 35; organization of, for proposal writing, 21-22
Institution: capability of, in proposal, 23-24; 48-49; mission of, and external funds, 20-21, 92-93; organizational relationships in, 24, 47-48; project management by, 79-87
Intergovernmental Cooperation Act of 1968, 106
Invitation for bids (IFB): in contracting, 96-97, 107-108; defined, 126; and guidelines, 126

J

Joint Funding Simplification Act of 1974, 106

K

Kellogg, W. K., 90
Kellogg Foundation, 38, 90-91, 116
Kiritz, N. J., 53
Knowledge, third user of, 91-92, 127
Knox, A. B., 3
Krathwohl, D. R., 53
Krebs, R. E., 87
Kurzig, C. M., 31, 39, 72, 73, 74-75, 77

L

Laboratory Animal Welfare Act of 1966, 111
Lefferts, R., 40, 74, 76, 77
Lenz, E., 93, 94
Leslie, J. W., 87
Letter of credit, 126
Letter of intent, 126

Liggett, T. C., 1-2, 29-40, 71n, 72
Local government: as funding source,
30; procedures of, 67-69
Lockheed Information Systems (LIS)
(DIALOG), 35, 36, 37

M

Madonna College, 38
Malo, P., 73, 77
Management, of funded projects,
79-87
Matching contributions: in budgets,
61-62; defined, 126
Matelski, S. M., 2, 80, 97, 103-114
Mawby, R. G., 91, 94
Maybee, R. G., 1, 2, 5-18, 41-53, 71n,
74
Mayor, R. A., 76, 77
Michigan State University, Extension
Service Program of, 90-91
Miles, M. B., 79, 81, 85, 87
Mindell, D., 79, 87
Minnesota, University of, Center for
Continuation Study of, 90
Mission statement: defined, 20; and
external funds, 92-93; for proposal
writing, 20-21
Montana, P., 86
Mueller, C., 123
Multiplier effect: analysis of, 89-94;
concept of, 89-90, 126; examples of,
90-91, 92; and third user of knowl-
edge, 91-92, 127
Mundel, J., 76, 77

N

Narrative: in proposal, 45-46; stan-
dard components for, 22-25
National Council on the Humanities,
67
National Endowment for the Hu-
manities, 66-67
Nebraska, University of, 82
Need, defined, 10
Needs assessment: defined, 126; in
proposal development, 8, 10, 23,
49-50
Nelson, C., 62
New York Community Trust, 76
Northwest Area Foundation, 34

O

Objective: defined, 42; in mission
statement, 20
Office of Federal Procurement Policy
(OFPP), 107
Office of the General Counsel, 114
ORBIT, 35, 36
Organization, temporary, 79-87
Overhead, 126

P

Pinnock, T. J., 89, 90, 94
Pledges: defined, 126; and tax ad-
vantages, 120
Principal investigator, 127
Priorities, 127
Process: defined, 7; overview of, 7-8;
for proposal development, 5-18
Procurement contracts, 109
Program officer, 15, 127
Program-planning-budgeting-system
(PPBS), for time allocation, 57
Project director, 15, 127
Project period, 125
Projects, sponsored: accounting information for, 82-83; analysis of
management of, 79-87; budget expenditures of, 84-85; cash flow
problems of, 84-85; communications from, 83-84; coordination of,
83-85; defined, 127; extension of,
86; interim project report on, 84;
organizing for, 81-83; permanent
files of, 86; planning for, 79-81;
staffing for, 81; termination of,
85-86
Proposals: activities diagram in, 24-
25; appeal process for, 14, 69;
authorization for, 11-12, 13; budget
standard components for, 25-26;
characteristics of, to foundations,
74-75; collaboration for, 10; concept
development phase of, 8-12; continuity for, 50, 51-52; criteria for,
41-42; criteria for, by foundations,
75-76; defined, 127; failure of,
69-70; and foundations, 71-77;
functions of, 41; funding agency
review phase of, 8-9, 14-16; goals-
objectives-activities in, 42-43; for
government agencies, 63-70; group